ONLY
GOOD THINGS

ONLY GOOD THINGS

Segments of a Memoir

Debra A. Baker

gatekeeper press
Columbus, Ohio

This book is a work of non-fiction. The names, characters and events in this book are the products of the author's best recall based on personal experiences. Any similarity to persons unrelated to actual encounters with the author whether real persons living or dead is coincidental and not intended by the author. In most cases, first names only are used to protect and respect privacy.

Only Good Things: Segments of a Memoir

Published by Gatekeeper Press
2167 Stringtown Rd, Suite 109
Columbus, OH 43123-2989
www.GatekeeperPress.com

Library of Congress Control Number: 2021932519

ISBN (hardcover): 9781662910333
eISBN: 9781662910340

Foreword

Thirty years ago, when I began writing this as my very first book, I thought long and hard about the interviews I would need to conduct to get the story across to readers. What I didn't realize is that no interviews would be necessary. God would provide enough material in my own life for my story. Good, bad, indifferent...didn't matter. There are so many good things in life that happen to each of us. However, life is not designed for good things only. Hardships and heartaches also happen. Why? They must; otherwise we are not living life to its full potential. And suffering, as hard as it is, brings us closer to God...always.

I dedicate this book to my late husband, Harry, and my two loving children, Harry III and Courtney – the guardians of my heart.

Contents

CHAPTER **1**

Sacred Relationships

There is no higher or more sacred relationship than the one I have with God, our Father. However, I do believe He has given me other relationships in my life that are precious and revered, true gifts directly from Him. These relationships are sacred in the way God has asked us to love one another as He has loved us. I try not to take these people for granted; I love them unconditionally and avail myself to their needs. These relationships are far from perfect, but there are true lessons I have learned from them over the years, and continue to learn.

I was just fourteen years old and in eighth grade during the New York State teachers' strike of the early 1970s. At that time, teachers were striking for a stronger voice in educational policy. The strike caused a tremendous workload for the teachers who crossed the picket line, and it doubled the size of the classrooms for several weeks.

One morning in the midst of a chaotic homeroom class, an African American girl who I thought at the time was a friend approached me with a wide smile. "He likes you!" she said with a wide grin and giggle. "He wants to talk to you!"

"Who?" I replied with irritation. "What are you talking about?"

"The tall, black, skinny one. The basketball player, Harry."

At that age, I was clearly what you would call a nerd. I didn't have too many friends, was a target for the bullies at the lunch table to pick on, and was happier doing homework than playing with the other kids. Need I say more? I let her comment go in one ear and out the other as I rolled my eyes in compete disgust. Little did I know at that time that she had approached Harry and said the same to him about me. An instigator at best.

The homeroom was a gathering place for students before the start of the day. Attendance was taken and announcements made, and then students would scatter to their first period class. Harry and I wouldn't have ended up in the same homeroom if not for the teacher's strike. A few days passed, and here came Miss Instigator hovering over my desk. "Here, he wants you to wear this," she said as she shoved a beautiful black and gold watch in front of my nose.

"What? I can't wear this!" I replied.

Just as I was about to get up from my chair to gain distance from her, I saw a tall, dark figure approach from the corner of my eye. Harry cleared his throat as he said, "Can I please have my watch back? It's my dad's."

Harry seemed a bit embarrassed, so I tried to ease the tension by saying, "It's a beautiful watch."

"Thanks. I can't go home without it," Harry retorted with a slight grin.

As Harry walked away, I think it was the first time I actually took full notice. He certainly was tall, and so, so thin. He had a neatly groomed close-cut afro that framed his tiny face. His eyes were brown and his nose was long and thin. He was neatly dressed in knit pants, a sweater and sneakers. And that grin – it lit up the room.

Shortly after the attempted matchmaking, I was walking down the hall struggling to carry my books for all my classes. Most kids carried a couple of books at a time and went back and forth to their locker, but not me; I had books and notepads for all eight periods ready to go at a moment's notice. Harry appeared out of nowhere and asked if I needed help carrying everything. After an initial hesitation, I acquiesced and let him help me, which quickly became a daily routine.

One day as we were walking down the hallway, he pointed to his denim jacket with the letters "D.R." embroidered on the back. "Did you notice?" he stated with determination. "I had your initials put on my jacket."

I turned and looked at the big red letters. "Wow, why did you do that?" I asked, not really sure what to expect.

"I don't know," he replied. "I thought it would be cool."

So, Harry continued to show up to carry my books, walk me to class, and then come by the lunch table to sit and talk. Before you knew it, the bullies had started to fade away, so I thought this actually was not a bad thing. I remember the day Harry asked me to be his girlfriend, as it was on my older sister's birthday in 1973. We were walking down the hallway as usual and he said, "Hey, how about you and me, one-on-one?" I was fourteen years old at the time, and little did I know I had found the person I would marry, be intimate and have children with, and share a life of great joys and sorrows.

We became known as a couple, and I started to attend his basketball games and cheer him on. He was an exceptional player, and the team relied on him heavily for his slam dunks and block shots. After one game, I waited for him to come out of the locker room. His guy friends were waiting too. I can remember all the nicknames they were shouting as he happily ran out the locker door: "Way to go, Slam Dunk!" "Great game, Rubberman!" "You got 'em, Doc!" I understood the first two nicknames, as he was known for his dunk shots and he was double jointed – but why Doc? It turned out it was his favorite professional basketball player, Julius Erving or the famous "Dr. J." I whipped my head around to look at him dead in the eyes. "And the D.R. on your jacket," I said without hesitation. "Was that for Dr. J too?"

He looked at me with eyes as big as buttons and then looked at the floor as he said, "Yeah, I guess it is." Well, I didn't let him forget about that for an awfully long time – if ever!

It was about eight months after he asked me out that I introduced him to my mom and Nana Grace, my grandmother, after a school play. Of course, I did receive the lecture from my mom about no dating until I was sixteen. Harry continued to call the house and we would be on the phone for hours. He started to ride his bike all the time from his home to mine, about five miles. Mom and Dad liked Harry, so over the next few years he became a staple in our household. After we married, my mom confided in me that he was around our house so much, she thought sometimes that she had borne him!

One particular day in middle school, Harry approached me with a huge grin as I was pulling books from my locker. He seemed to be in a great mood that day. "And how are you doing today?" he stated, peering down over me with one hand leaning on the locker next to mine and the other hidden behind his hip. He was 6'4" to my 5'6", so I was used to looking upward to talk with him.

"I'm good," I responded with a shy smile. "And you?"

He moved his hand from behind his hip and displayed a tiny, neatly wrapped box. *Wow* was my first thought. He had completely surprised me. I quickly threw my books back into the locker to free my hands to open the package. As I unwrapped the tiny box, I felt my heart race. *What could this possibly be?* I thought. Inside was a beautiful necklace, a small glass ball in the middle and a tiny seed inside the ball. I looked at him and said, "Thank you. It's beautiful."

"It's a mustard seed. I'm happy you like it," Harry softly replied. I turned my back to him so he could help with the clasp. I wanted to wear it right away. I didn't know at the time what the significance of a mustard seed was, but it felt special just for receiving it as my very first gift from a boyfriend. I wore the mustard seed every day for a very long time. I found out the true meaning of that gift some 40 years later.

Over the years, Harry continued to bury himself in basketball and I in my books. On the outside we looked quite incompatible. However, on the inside our spirits were aligned—we believed in the same things, we shared the same goals, we cared about our family and friends, and most importantly we had our faith. We stayed together throughout junior high and high school; I was the quiet, shy bookworm, he was the tall, talented basketball player. Since we lived in different sections of town, we were forced to attend different junior high schools. It was for only one year, but it was my worst year in my entire school history. I just didn't want to be there without Harry.

In 1975, Harry and I were rejoined in high school. He continued to excel at basketball, and I focused on my academics. Soon it was time to pick colleges, and Harry had his pick of many schools that wanted to recruit him for basketball, but he was keen to select one where he thought he could survive academically. At that time, he was also interested in auto mechanics, so the school had to have that program as well, and he eventually settled on a college in Montana. I, on the other hand, desperately wanted to go to college for the academics. My parents were raising four children, so I knew I would have to pay for most of my tuition through loans, work-study and savings. I was interested in tourism and trade at the time, so I wanted a school that had that program, and found it at Niagara University (NU), a small private Catholic university in upstate New York. The odd thing is that I showed up without ever visiting the campus, just relying on the brochure and information pack.

It fit into exactly what I felt I wanted and needed in a university. I must admit, it was difficult at times trying to maintain my relationship with my boyfriend for the next four years and across 1,900 miles. But we did it. We would write often, have our weekly calls, and see each other over the summers. We were each other's sounding boards, a safe place to share our insecurities and worries. I left for my freshman year first, while Harry had a couple of weeks before venturing to Montana. Our last night together we had a spectacular dinner, told each other how much we loved each other, then took a $1 bill and professed our love on it. We vowed to do that each year we were apart and to keep it to show our children that we made it through! We used a $5 bill the next year, then a $10 bill, and finally a $20 bill our senior year. They continue to be framed behind a picture of my husband posing in his Montana basketball uniform with a full smile, and I treasure that memory to this day.

Basketball went fine for Harry for the first couple of years, but by his junior year there was increasing pressure for him to perform, and his relationship with his coaches started to falter. He started to gain weight and the school was on him to lose it fast. For me school was going fine, however I changed my major after my freshman year to economics, which added additional stress to catch up. I had to lean on my friendships with Dietra and Kareen as we became good friends over the years. Dietra was from Buffalo and Kareen was from Queens, and we bonded in all aspects—we were all young Catholic girls, we all had conservative views on sex, relationships and marriage, and we all had a desire to do as much as we could to make it better for the women and men of color who came after us.

Dietra had an athletic build, big beautiful brown eyes, and long brown hair which went down to her shoulders. She had a great sense of humor and an infectious laugh. Kareen had a lovely Haitian accent, was light-skinned, and had curves in all the right places. She spoke so rapidly that she often called Dietra and I "DebraDietra" so she didn't have to stop to figure out who was who. Dietra loves telling the story how she rescued me freshman year. We lived in Walker Hall which was a dorm about a mile off campus. We hardly knew one another but bonded by sight, because of being two African American women at this college which had very few. One early evening she knocked on my dorm door and opened it wide, to find me sitting at my desk in my pajamas sobbing. "Hey, what's the matter with you?" she said with confusion.

Through my sobs I replied, "I miss my boyfriend."

"Oh, stop it," she stated matter-of-factly. "Wipe your face and get dressed. We're going out." The bonding began.

Dietra, Kareen and I decided to be roommates our sophomore year, and settled on Room 626 in one of the more modern dorms on campus. This was a triple room and we decorated it in a homey, comfortable feel. There was an antechamber as soon as you walked in the door, in which we placed two wooden desks side by side with chairs, a microwave oven, a stereo set and a coffee maker. Inside the larger room was a single bed against one wall and a set of bunk beds against the other. A desk sat under the window overlooking campus. We shared the two closets and kept the room in good order. Most nights Kareen would put on an Earth, Wind & Fire album so we could fall asleep to smooth, soothing music. Kareen was studying nursing, Dietra was studying communications and I was now studying economics.

I have very fond memories of Room 626—it was our sanctuary, our safe haven, our home—but by junior year I had become interested in becoming a resident assistant (RA). This had multiple benefits as it would help defray some of my tuition costs, and also allow me to get a single room. This would also give me an opportunity to meet more people on campus and help others. Worked for me – on to the next adventure! It was hard leaving Dietra and Kareen, but I knew we would still remain close friends even if we didn't room together. And we did.

There was a small group of people of color at NU at the time, strategizing to form the school's first Minority Cultural Society. This occurred in the early 1980s, before the focus on diversity and inclusion came into full force.

These dozen people formed a coalition in order to bring awareness to the different needs of people of color on campus, and Dietra, Kareen and I knew we had a role to play. Each of us had a story and came from different backgrounds. Some of our friends in the coalition were attending college as part of a needs-based program called the Niagara University Opportunity Program. At that time, I did not fully understand the power and necessity of initiating a group focused on these issues, but Dietra, Kareen and I would often sit in our dorm room and discuss ways we could make things better for people like us. There was this common bond, and I was so blessed to have Dietra and Kareen in my life guiding, educating and caring for me and others.

During my senior year at NU, I was selected as one of three students in contention for a highly regarded economics award voted on by the faculty, but the award ceremony was on the same night as an end-of-year celebration for our Minority Cultural Society. I remember speaking to Dietra about the conflict and how disappointed I was to miss our celebration. Dietra replied, "Nonsense. You worked very hard for this, and I'll be sitting right by your side when they announce your name for the economics award!" And sure enough, Dietra did attend that ceremony in that round lecture room with me.

When the announcer stated, "And the award goes to Jeffrey!" and I felt my eyes begin to well, it wasn't because I didn't win the award. I was upset because I had given up a night to celebrate some great accomplishments with my friends in the Minority Cultural Society, and the cause was so much bigger than any one award. I had just wasted my time; and more importantly, Dietra's time. I felt Dietra's eyes look at me as she sat in the seat to my right. She put her hand on my arm and whispered, "It's okay, Deb, you've already won." There was a reception afterwards but Dietra and I didn't go, but rather slipped out and ran across the campus to be with our friends. We were seniors and wanted to celebrate the accomplishments of the Society.

The next day, my economics professor approached me and inquired as to why I had not attended the reception, and I told him I had something particularly important I had to do. He took my not attending as a reaction to not getting the award, but it was quite the opposite. I think God was making sure I could be where I was most needed. My friends would have deeply missed celebrating with me, but I'm not so sure the multitude of faculty and other guests at that awards gathering would've felt the same.

Junior year was definitely a pivotal point for Harry and me. He was not happy with school and basketball, and I was trying to establish myself as a competent RA. I would say, in all our dating life, this is the period I felt most disconnected. I was trying to empathize but at that time didn't understand there was very little I could do for Harry; he had to do it himself. I could have prayed more for him, though; that's always something we can do for another person, especially when they're challenged.

Harry and I talked about him transferring to my college, but in hindsight this probably would've made a bad situation worse.

I poured my heart and soul into the RA job. It was so much better than my previous campus jobs, and I was grateful to have it. Not working wasn't an option – I had to work during college to ensure my bills would be paid at the end of the semester, and I took my campus jobs very seriously, knowing that completing my education depended on it. At the time I attended NU, there was a no co-ed policy, which meant men and women could not have visitation rights in each other's dorm room unless there was a specified university event. One of my jobs as a RA was to report any instances of illegal visitation. As you can imagine, this didn't make me the most popular gal on campus.

With senior year approaching, the university did not have a Resident Director candidate, who would be the leader for all the RAs. I was approached and asked to consider becoming their first Acting Resident Director (ARD), as a full Director was typically a graduate student. I was thrilled. This would entitle me to more pay and a private suite on campus. I moved into a more historic dorm on campus my senior year and began the job. As you walked down the first floor of the dorm, the room was on the left side and took up half the hallway. My new suite was like a mini apartment, including a separate office apart from the living room with cathedral ceilings, a mini kitchen area, and a nice sized bedroom area that could comfortably fit two beds. The windows were arched and beautiful. On quiet days, you could open one and hear the water from the gorge across the street.

This job required more responsibility and was more demanding on my time. The extended RA team was a group of lively, smart women who worked hard at both school and work. We became remarkably close and had to deal with fire alarms, dorm policy changes and the like; but most importantly, we were there for the students who needed support in all areas of their life. The most difficult part of my tenure as ARD was one evening towards the end of senior year, when I called Harry sobbing uncontrollably. I needed a friend; no, I needed *my* friend. My very best friend on Earth.

At the end of my senior year, I was sitting on my bed in my dorm suite one late night when the telephone rang. It was the Dean of Men, asking if we had a student in our dorm named Lisa. I replied, "Yes, she lives here on the first floor." He asked me to lay the phone down, go to her room and check that she was there. I did as he said, but her room was dark, the twin beds unmade, nothing looking unusual. When I told him, he sent a car around to take me to the local hospital to meet him. He grabbed my arm when I arrived and said, "There's been a terrible accident. We need you to let us know if you recognize this person as Lisa. Her grandparents are local so we called them and they are here, but we don't want them to see her in this condition."

I knew Lisa fairly well, average height and brunette wavy hair with a beautiful smile. I couldn't bear to think of my grandparents ever having to see me on my death bed. But I wasn't prepared for what was to come. Lisa had been in a car accident during an evening out.

I entered the room timidly. Lisa was lying on the bed, her body swollen from the accident, but I knew it was her. I turned to the dean, shook my head affirmatively and raced across the hall to the bathroom, gasping and feeling nauseous. I will never forget that night, and I will never forget Lisa. After that evening, I knew it was time to graduate and return home, as I could not get that last image of Lisa out of my head. I had such wonderful memories at NU and was saddened to have it end this way. I called my very best friend in the world and laid all this on him. He helped me make it through that difficult night. What I didn't realize at that time is the sacredness of being in the presence of someone who is passing or has just passed to external life. Lisa was my first experience; however, there were more to come. And yes, it's still a frightful, agonizing experience. However, I'm learning to surround those feelings with intentional, deep, solemn prayer.

After this tragic experience, I focused on graduation and moving back home with my family. I think there may be very few people who can say a saint was the keynote speaker at their college graduation ceremony; but while Mother Teresa of Calcutta had not yet been canonized as a saint during Niagara University's graduation in 1982, she's now known as Saint Teresa of Calcutta. There were many aspects of her graduation speech I feel I've tried to live by, and especially as she spoke about life and family, which touches my heart to this day:

You are going out. You will meet suffering. You will meet humiliation. You will meet sorrow. You will meet joy. You will meet success. You will be wanted. You will be unwanted. You will be loved. You will not be loved. All that is part of Jesus' fate. "Pick up the cross and follow me." "And follow me." We don't have to go ahead of Him. And to be able to do that, He has made Himself bread of life, to give us life, to satisfy our hunger for God. And then He makes himself the hungry One, so that you and I can satisfy His hunger for our love. So, it is wonderful when we come to know that Love. Again I say, love begins at home. The family that prays together, stays together. And if you stay together, you will love one another as Jesus loves each one of us.

I stand in awe of the worldly positive impact and experiences of Saint Teresa of Calcutta; however, while she was busy doing the Lord's work, I'm sure a part of her needed fellowship with people on Earth. As much as we must turn to God for our every need, God also designed us for fellowship, not only with God but also with other brothers and sisters in Christ.

Seven years after college graduation, Harry and
I married. It was almost sixteen years in the making! I was
beginning to think we were never going to get married.
My dad had stressed to me that we had to "get off the
pot" if we were serious, so just prior to our engagement
Harry and I had a heart-to-heart discussion. I shared
that I was disappointed in this stage of our relationship,
and he shared that the timing of giving me the ring was
never right – we were either too busy with our jobs or
disconnected on some minor issue. I was waiting for
Harry to be my husband before giving myself fully to a
man. I needed reassurance that he felt I was the forever
one for him.

The Christmas after that conversation, Harry stopped
by our former middle school on the way to Christmas
dinner at Aunt Mary and Uncle Bob's house. He drove
up to the front of the school and explained there was
a basketball trophy in the window in his honor. We
hurried out of the car and up the front steps dressed in
our Christmas best. It was a cold, crisp, beautiful day.
The sun was shining brightly and there was a fresh smell
in the air. Harry stopped suddenly when we reached the
top step. He turned to me and said, "This is where it all
started." He bent down on one knee and reached into his
coat pocket to deliver a ring box. He looked me in the
eyes and said, "Will you be my wife, you and me, one-
on-one forever?" I felt the warm tears streaming down my
cold face. This is what I had waited so long to hear. This

was what I had dreamt about for so many years. I looked into his eyes and said, "Yes, always and forever yours."

We had purchased our first home two years prior to our wedding date, and was working hard within our respective careers. Harry landed a job working for New York State, first in youth services and later for the Department of Corrections. My college roommate Kareen reached out to her mom, Josephine, to secure an interview for me at a financial services firm in New York City. And so our career journeys began. We married and then two years later our first child was born, Harry III, but not before moving into our second home (a mile up the hill) when I was five months pregnant. There was no discussion on the name. Ever since we had been 16 years old, Harry had made it quite clear if he ever had a son, he must carry on the name, full stop. I call our son "HJ" for Harry Jr. even though he's technically not a junior, my husband was. What a joy and a special gift that HJ was born on my birthday! We call it the "10-14 factor;" whenever we start to think alike or arrive at the same conclusion, we look at each other and simply say "10-14!"

For a long time, I dreamt about carrying a baby in my belly and could not wait to experience the joy and wonder. This did not happen for me until I was in my early thirties. When I was a very young girl, I thought every woman was born with a baby already in their tummy. As the woman grew, the baby grew too! I would sit and rock my baby and truly believed there was something inside there. It was an innocent childhood fantasy, but what a beautiful way to honor motherhood.

In the winter of 1991, I was beginning to feel very tired and bloated. I took an at-home pregnancy test that confirmed we were expecting a bundle of joy. I checked the time; it was 6:00 a.m. on a weekday morning. Harry was in bed sound asleep on one of his few days off. I was dressed and getting ready to head to the train station for the daily commute to work. *Do I wake him and tell him or wait until I get home tonight?*

I tiptoed over to the bed with the positive pregnancy stick in hand. I shook him. Nothing. I shook him again. He opened one eye and gruffly said, "What is it Deb?"

I shoved the pregnancy test in front of his one open eye. "We're pregnant!"

Harry looked at me in sheer confusion. "Are you sure? Absolutely sure?"

"Yup, we're going to have a baby," I replied with absolute glee.

Harry kissed and hugged me, and off I went to work. It wasn't until I came home later that evening when he timidly asked me, "Did you wake me up and say we're having a baby, or did I dream that?"

All was going well with my first pregnancy until the beginning of the ninth month, when I developed severe high blood pressure and sugar levels. I had to be hospitalized for the last couple weeks of the pregnancy. I was sad and distraught as there were still things to do in preparing for the baby. I left work sooner than planned, the nursery was not ready, and we had just moved into a new home that still needed to be organized.

The phone rang in the hospital room and it was Aunt Mary. "Well, hello Deb," she said. "How are you feeling today?"

Out of nowhere, I began to cry. Aunt Mary continued, "Everything's going to be wonderful. Try to keep yourself busy and the time will fly by quickly. This is all for the best, Deb. And when you hold that little baby in your arms for the first time, you will not remember any of this."

Shortly after that phone call, the doctor arrived at my bedside. "Well, if you don't go into labor over the weekend, we'll induce on Monday, okay?" he said.

Without hesitation, I replied, "Yes, that sounds great."

After the doctor left the room, my husband looked at me and said, "You do know what Monday is, don't you?"

I paused to think and then said, "No, what's Monday?"

My husband shook his head side to side and said, "It's your birthday, Deb!"

HJ has a very easygoing personality, and has grown into a strong young man. He takes life with happiness and ease, loves people, and has a sense of God's strength and will. I remember when he was about one month old, dear Aunt Mary came to visit us. She looked over at him lying and cooing in his bassinet and said, "He looks like he's saying, 'Okay, world, I'm here, now give me some love!'" That still brings a smile to my face, twenty-nine years later, and I think HJ is still saying that!

One day when HJ was about ten years old, we were out doing errands and on our last stop I dragged him into a clothing store with me, as I needed a work outfit pronto. I explained to him that I needed this outfit for an important presentation that Mom had to do. As I was looking quickly through the suits, my son picked one up and held it out to me, saying, "Here you go, Mom. This would look nice on you." I looked down at his ballplayer hands holding the bold red suit and started to smile. I bent over and hugged him as I gently put the suit back on the rack. I said, "Honey, Mom has never worn a red suit to work. In my business it means you're powerful, and I'm just not ready for that!" We both had a good chuckle and I ended up with my typical black suit that looked like the other ten I had at home in the closet. It was not until I retired, fifteen years after that shopping spree, while relaxing and conversing at home with my adult children, feeling a sense of gratefulness for my new freedom, that I realized there was nothing holding me back from getting that red suit now.

Nearly five years after the birth of HJ, our second blessing came with the birth of our daughter, Courtney. As I sit here and write this, I am overwhelmed by these two children who have been my saving grace, and God's precious gifts to us. Courtney is a darling and has always been the most serious and studious one of the family. During my entire pregnancy with her, my husband thought we were having another boy, and he was shocked upon delivery that it was a girl. I think that's why he was so very protective of her; she was truly the apple of his eye, and based on her personality there was no denying they shared DNA. When she was a preteen, someone gave me the book A *Purpose Driven Life* by Rick Warren. I mentioned to her in passing that I was too busy working at the moment and didn't have time to read it. One evening when I came home from work, the book was on the table with crib notes next to it. Courtney had read as much as she could, then typed crib notes so I would understand the gist. At the end of the book, she inserted a handwritten note that said: "When done put something at end of each week." She is simply amazing.

My daughter is actually the one who had to educate me on different aspects of prejudice, racism and diversity. I've been discriminated against in my life, and know the feeling of being judged by your appearance; however, I did not fully understand the hidden levels of racism that still exist in our nation. The school systems in our neighborhood were widely known for being one of the best for our area. What I didn't realize is those statistics never account for placing African American children in our neighborhood schools that were predominantly white. Courtney has been an activist for change and the underserved since middle school. She has taught all of us how to check our perceptions versus reality, and how to become educated on the multicultural, multigenerational, multi-language issues that our children face today.

She has also actively dealt with stress, anxiety and depression. She has been a role model to me. She admits to having tendencies of a high-stressed individual and a perfectionist at times. I know I was not a good example of how to deal with this when she was a young girl. This worried her father to such a point that one day he said to her, "Court, you have to protect yourself and just let certain things go. Sometimes we have to take off the rose-colored glasses and see things for what they really are." That was unacceptable to our Courtney. You don't accept things for what they are…you change them to make it better.

HJ played sports most of his school years, mainly basketball and football. He graduated from Penn State University at State College, while Courtney was always an advocate for human rights and education and graduated from Brown University in Providence, Rhode Island. I am immensely proud of both our children, and I will leave the emotional space for them to one day write their own stories if they so choose. I do understand they're precious gifts from God, and I thank God for them. Every. Single. Day.

> *"If I speak in the tongues of men and of angels, but have not love, I am a noisy gong or a clanging cymbal. And if I have prophetic powers, and understand all mysteries and all knowledge, and if I have all faith, so as to remove mountains, but have not love, I am nothing. If I give away all I have, and if I deliver up my body to be burned, but have not love, I gain nothing. Love is patient and kind; love does not*

envy or boast; it is not arrogant or rude. It does not insist on its own way; it is not irritable or resentful; it does not rejoice at wrongdoing, but rejoices with the truth. Love bears all things, believes all things, hopes all things, endures all things." (1 Corinthians 13:1-7, Holy Bible English Standard Version [ESV])

CHAPTER 2

Unkept Promises

Whirling down the hill going around the bend, I can still see the sleek white hair, worn face and wide smile of my neighbor George, throwing up his hand to wave hello as I drove by his home. I quickly slowed down to stop and say hello. George rapidly approached my window while looking behind my car to ensure we were safe to have our quick conversation. "How ya doing?" George belted out with that big, beautiful smile. Before I could respond, he added, "How's Harry and the kids?" George was in his mid-fifties when we first met some thirty years ago. A slender 5'8", he had aged with grace and looked fit and healthy. His usual attire was jeans, a checkered work shirt, boots, and gloves in hand. He was married to a wonderful, quiet, kind woman named Rose. She had been battling cancer for some time; however, when I met her she was in remission.

Rose was truly a woman of grace and dignity. She, like George, was tiny in frame and mighty in heart. Her brown hair framed her tiny face and was always neat and done up. She often wore khakis, a starched cotton shirt and flats. Like George, she had a gentle, peaceful smile and spoke with a refreshing soft voice. She loved her family dearly, as was evidenced in the amount of time and help she provided to them.

Many years ago, George owned his own sanitation company, which is how my husband and I first met him. At that time we were living in our first home that we loved, a small two- bedroom, two-story house in Marlboro, New York. George's company would collect our trash once a week. When I was pregnant with our first child, HJ, my husband and I started to look for a bigger home. We settled one mile up the hill. Unbeknownst to us at the time, this was two houses away from George and Rose, who had lived there an exceptionally long time.

My husband and I searched for our first home for a couple of years before settling in Marlboro, which is about ten miles north from where we grew up in Newburgh, New York, me in the suburbs and my husband in the inner city. After dating for fifteen and a half years, we were hopeful we were destined for marriage; and as type-A personalities, we wanted to try to buy a house as we planned our married life together. There was no argument that we would stay in the beautiful Hudson Valley, although as a child I didn't appreciate it as I do now. I know living here has been a true blessing.

George and Rose's home was a lovely blue ranch that sat on a small hill. All the activity seemed to be through their garage door that faced the street. I don't ever recall seeing anyone go in or out of their front door. They were both previously married and had children from those marriages. Their grandson Tyler, who spent a lot of time at "Pop's" house, became an incredibly good friend and schoolmate to our son Harry, so there was a great connection to George and Rose through him. My son tells me about when all the boys would be up the street at their friend Garrett's house (about six houses from George's house), and all of a sudden Tyler would jump up and say, "I gotta go! Pop is calling me for supper!" The other kids would look at each other and shrug their shoulders, as they had not heard a thing. Sure enough, Tyler would run down the street and there would be George in the driveway, waiting for him to come inside to have dinner. Amazing.

One year we invited George and Rose along with some other neighbors, family, and friends to one of our famous Fourth of July parties. I was pregnant with our first son for our inaugural party, wearing a green shirt that said "Dallas" stretched across my chest and my husband matching, both shirts of which had been picked up at the airport after once returning home from a business trip. Everyone would bring delicious side dishes and desserts to the "Bakers' Fourth of July party" and we would grill hot dogs, hamburgers, chicken, ribs and sometimes fish. And yes, let's not forget the ample amount of beer and wine! These parties were held for several years in a row and got bigger and better with time.

One year I came out the back door with arms full of dishes to serve, and just stopped dead in my tracks. I realized that there were some folks in the yard I didn't know. I looked around and had an out-of-body experience. *Is this our party? How do we control all this? I've got to get around and meet everyone!* And the most touching observation was to experience diversity at its best. I gave a big sigh and thought to myself, *this is what it's supposed to be like in this world.* Everyone was having a great time and it didn't matter where you lived, the color of your skin, your social status in the world—not a thing. What mattered was that you were there to have fun, meet new friends, and share in fellowship and friendship.

After spending some time with our immediate next-door neighbors, the Parks, we quickly learned that they were related to George and Rose. In fact, they informed us that we were now living in their Uncle Jim and Aunt Ruth's house. To top it off, Uncle Jim and Aunt Ruth still lived in Marlboro—a few houses behind their original house that we now occupied! We later learned that we had purchased what was originally farmland, owned by one of the longstanding Italian families in Marlboro. At that time there were not that many African Americans living in Marlboro, and we were so grateful to feel welcomed by our neighbors and to have them truly treat us as extended family members.

At one of the Fourth of July parties, I noticed my dad with this big smile on his face. He was walking towards George as he entered the backyard. They embraced as they patted each other on the back. I could see them talking and laughing. My dad was a friendly guy, but

I was quite surprised at the embrace. I could clearly see they knew each other and were happy to see each other. I later found out that my dad and George both worked at a well-known automobile manufacturing company and knew each other from there. Small world, or so I thought.

Rose's cancer eventually came back, and she passed in 2011. George was devastated. She was his true love. He kept himself busy with his children, grandchildren, lawn work, and working at the local landfill as a Department Head. One day I ran into George at the local market in town and asked how he was doing. "It's very lonely without Rose," he replied with sadness. I felt empathy for him. My heart was truly aching. "Why don't you come to dinner," I blurted. He then said, "Everyone invites me to dinner, but I can't just show up. There has to be a certain day and time, you know?" Of course, I told him I would contact him with all the details.

Weeks, months and years passed. Busyness filled my days. The invite was never sent. One night after arriving home late from work, I had barely sat down in the chair when my husband told me George had died. As was typical with George, he was doing lawn work and died of an apparent heart attack. I immediately thought about all those times I had reminded myself to get George that date and time for dinner. It never came. It saddened me to think I did not prioritize my good neighbor and friend, George.

"...you shall love the Lord your God with all your heart and with all your soul and with all your mind. This is the great and first commandment. And a second is like it: You shall love your neighbor as yourself. On these two commandments depend all the Law and the Prophets." (Matthew 22:37-40, ESV)

In order to love others, you must love God first. When I am loving God more than anything else, I can then love others. I know in my heart that the problem wasn't I was too busy. I could have easily made time for George and met his need for connection and fellowship by getting back to him with the details for dinner. The problem was that I was so focused on my plans, my agenda and my to-do lists, I couldn't see the importance of taking the time to spend with George. I had taken my eyes off of loving God fully and placed it on myself. I was finding joy in my accomplishments and reaching for what I perceived as the next best career journey, instead of being there for a friend and neighbor in need. George simply wanted me to care. He just wanted an escape from the abyss of loneliness he had lived with every day since Rose had passed. George was my neighbor. He geographically lived next to me, but had I really loved him as my neighbor?

In the above verse from the Book of Matthew, it is not enough to love people who are near to me. How many people in my church do I truly love? Do I take the time to love others who are geographically close but emotionally distant? What constitutes a "neighbor" has nothing to do with the physical location of that person relative to you. It's much more far-reaching. That encounter with George changed my perspective on how to love others. I had wasted so much time focusing on myself and what I wanted, I had not prioritized what George needed from me. Maybe I couldn't give him a material or a permanent solution to his loneliness, but I could've allowed him to bend my ear for a while. I could have laughed at his jokes and listened to his stories about how he had met and fell in love with Rose. I could have listened to every detail. I could have reminded him about all those times it was snowing up to our knees and he ensured that our weekly trash was hauled away. I could have listened when he described how much he loved to cook his favorite Italian dishes, and how he cared for Rose on days she was just too tired to do it all. But I didn't. And I missed out on a God ordained opportunity.

Sometimes all we can give people is ourselves. Peter and John experienced this:

> "And Peter directed his gaze at him, as did John, and said, 'Look at us.' And he fixed his attention on them, expecting to receive something from them. But Peter said, 'I have no silver and gold, but what I do have, I give to you. In the name of Jesus Christ of Nazareth, rise up and walk!'" (Acts 3:4-6, ESV)

Peter and John were ordinary, uneducated men. They had no money to give the lame stranger, but they had something more to share with him—themselves. Their experiences with the Holy Spirit were the key to this man's healing. He thought all he needed was money, but what he received was so much better. They gave him their attention. Verse 4 is quick to point out that "...Peter directed his gaze at him, as did John." A lame man at the temple was probably used to being ignored. Sitting at the temple gate begging every day earned him sneers and jeers from most regulars who frequently walked by him. But Peter and John do something different. They give him back his dignity. Peter and John could have walked right into the temple for prayer. They could have gone through the religious rituals by going to pray. But because of their love for God, they were able to be used by Him in an incredible way for the purpose of healing the man.

If you've ever missed out on an opportunity to be used by God for fulfilling a promise, there's hope. We serve a God of second—and a hundred—chances. That's a part of His grace. Although my unkept promise to George robbed me of the joy of God using me for His purposes, it didn't mean I was disqualified from being used by Him in the future. And for that, I am forever grateful.

My husband had been on dialysis for about eighteen months when he was finally cleared for a kidney transplant at a New York based hospital. He was also attempting to get clearance at a hospital in Florida at the same time. We were prepared to accept whatever offer came first. It was such an ordeal to get on the transplant list that I still cannot bring myself to delete the voicemail informing us that he was in "active status, level 1." Our niece, Gina, approached us about getting tested to be her uncle's living donor. We were shocked and beyond grateful that she would do this. They already had a special bond. When Gina was facing some challenging events in her own life, it was Uncle Harry who showed up at her doorstep and told her it was all going to be okay. He removed his cross necklace and placed it on her. He wanted her to have faith. She did just that and is our living angel today.

My husband arrived home from dialysis that day with super-high energy and enthusiasm. It had been a long road for him. He and Gina were scheduled to have the transplant on February 22nd which was a few days away. I greeted him at the door and said, "Well, hello there!" We were both on a high, and had a feeling that we had turned a major corner and were on our way. He barely took off his jacket before whipping out his cell phone and beginning to show me pictures he took on his last day at dialysis. There were shots of him with the staff members, other dialysis patients, and the facility. He stopped and lingered over one of a beautiful African American woman and man. She had soft brown eyes, a bright smile, and a glowing red silk shirt – but it was her hair that drew you in. The tightly wrapped white turban crossed at the forehead to allow her salt-and-pepper wavy hair to stand vertically on her head. She wore a beautiful gold necklace and large gold thick-looped earrings with diamond specks in them. Standing closely next to her, as though it was a continuation of the same person, was an African American man with sunshades, a beret-type hat, and a salt-and-pepper mustache and beard that didn't hide his grin of contentment. His blue shirt was just as bright as her red one, and he was nestled in his jacket as though he had just arrived or was about to leave.

"This is Nancy and Dio," I heard my husband say, almost in a whisper. "They're married." Turned out that Nancy was also a dialysis patient, and he said he had admired her from afar when he first started attending himself, because she carried herself with a sense of peace. She always had a pleasant smile, and was able to lift my husband's spirits effortlessly.

After they broke the ice with their initial conversations, they became fast friends. Nancy told Harry all about her husband Dio who she cherished, and her children and grandchildren. Harry's heart melted when he realized Nancy was much older than he, and was going through this same trauma. What was just as hard to digest was that her husband Dio had been battling cancer for many years. They were both faithful people and believed God would get them through any challenges this life brings them. When my husband passed, Nancy and Dio were at the funeral. I recognized them immediately from my husband's photo. They followed up weeks after with phone calls to see how my children and I were holding up.

Several weeks after my husband passed, Nancy called to say she had been selected to receive a kidney transplant. This was such good news! Nancy had her surgery a couple of months later. Soon thereafter, though, Dio called to let me know she was not faring too well or eating well, and with further testing she was diagnosed with cancer, passing away not long thereafter. Dio was truly devastated.

I was in Florida when the funeral date arrived, and I called Dio that morning. I told him that he was in my prayers and that I loved him. I asked him to remember that God is with us. When I returned home from Florida, I called Dio and asked if I could visit. He said he was weak and not feeling well but I could stop by for a short visit. I showed up at his home with food, a big hug and tears. We did not have to say much to one another as we both understood the deep grief of losing a spouse. I told Dio I was here for him and that I would continue to check in on him. And through prayers and guidance, I have been able to keep my word to Dio.

God places people in our lives for a reason, some for a season and some for a lifetime. Although it's hard to understand that sometimes; our instincts are to not want to love deeply, for fear if we love people in our lives they may leave us. George is a great example of that. If I had chosen to love him as my true neighbor, I would have been able to enjoy George's company and relish in the gift his presence provided in my life. I learned a valuable lesson and I am so happy God allowed me to enjoy the gift of loving neighbors through Nancy and Dio. Not only did they touch my life, but they deeply touched my husband's life as well, and he touched theirs.

CHAPTER 3

Mishpat

There was a fever pitch of excitement that filled the air at work in the late 1980s. I was a team leader for an analytics group at the second financial institution of my career. Part of my responsibilities was to support the sales teams in their efforts to sell our products. From time to time, big deals would come about, and everyone across the different product disciplines would clamor to be a part of it. It was an honor to be part of the deal team, and if done well it would lead to other career opportunities. I was fortunate enough to get on a particular deal team that had everyone in the division excited, because of the possibility that we could win over one of our competitors' larger corporate fund clients. All hands on deck! I put extra time and energy into this deal. I had just gotten engaged to my boyfriend of the last fifteen years, and knew that planning a wedding and working on this deal would be very stressful, but I was up for this challenge. Late-night briefings, presentation coordination, rehearsals; all the ingredients of winning a great deal were expected and executed from this deal team.

One day during preparations, my boss called me into her office. I jumped up with pen and paper in hand, eager to learn how she needed me and what great assignment was coming my way. Or perhaps she was going to thank me for putting so much time into the deal and give me the recognition and positive reinforcement that helps motivate real, hard work. I entered her office with a polite smile, and she asked me to close the door and take a seat in front of her desk. She was not smiling. She could barely keep eye contact with me. I had a good relationship with my boss. She was tough at times, but she drove me to do my best. She was in her mid-thirties, about 5'5", curvy and fit. She had beautiful green eyes, olive skin and short brown hair.

I heard myself talking before she had a chance to say anything, spilling out the words "what's wrong?" as though someone had just punched me in the stomach.

She looked up from her desk and said, "You won't be going to the presentation for the big deal. We had a meeting, and most people felt you would hurt more than help." Before I could get a word out, she continued, "...because you're Black." She could barely get the letters b-l-a-c-k out of her mouth before she began to cry uncontrollably. She started again. "Down South things are different than here, and the thought is that the prospective client would not appreciate you on the deal team," she stated through heaves and sobs.

I immediately got up from my chair and my instinct was to run out of that room, but I didn't. I walked around to her desk and held her tight. We cried together that day. I never mentioned the incident again to her, and I never told anyone at work the real reason I didn't go down South to present with the rest of the team. I held that all inside. It was the fuel I needed to understand what racism felt like. In my mind, I was going to do everything in my power to help women like me who don't get a chance to show their talents because of the color of their skin. I am still friends with that boss to this day, and she was a guest at my wedding. I never blamed the messenger, but the message was crystal clear.

"Now he was teaching in one of the synagogues on the Sabbath. And behold, there was a woman who had had a disabling spirit for eighteen years. She was bent over and could not fully straighten herself. When Jesus saw her, he called her over and said to her, 'Woman, you are freed from your disability.' And he laid his hands on her, and immediately she was made straight, and she glorified God. But the ruler of the synagogue, indignant because Jesus had healed on the Sabbath, said to the people, 'There are six days in which work ought to be done. Come on those days and be healed, and not on the Sabbath day.' Then the Lord answered him, 'You hypocrites! Does not each of you on the Sabbath untie his ox or his donkey from the manger and lead it away to water it? And ought not this woman, a daughter of Abraham whom Satan bound for eighteen years,

be loosed from this bond on the Sabbath day?' As
he said these things, all his adversaries were put to
shame, and all the people rejoiced at all the glorious
things that were done by him." (Luke 13:10-17, ESV)

Jesus was one of the most liberating people of his
time. Jesus knew the love of His Father, who said, "Male
and female he created them." God desires equality for
all His creation. Except, in this broken world we may not
always get it. Jesus's compassion outweighed his necessity
to observe the Sabbath. Jesus was keeping the spirit of the
Law, rather than the letter of it. His compassion for the
sick person trumped his need to observe cultural norms.

That deal team moment sticks out in my memory today.
I wish we could be more unified in society; however, it is
more divided than ever before. Black, White, Republican,
Democrat. Everyone is taking sides. Our wanting to
believe that another human being or condition could be
inferior to others is plain wrong. It skews our perceptions
of who people are. Just like the leader in this story from
Luke couldn't see Jesus for His compassion, but rather his
legalism regarding the Sabbath, those leaders on the deal
team could only see their preconceived ideas of Black
people being inferior to White. And the saddest thing
of all, they were not willing to think differently, make a
change for the better, or act like Jesus.

As Christians, I honestly believe we can change all
that. Think about the people whom God has placed
in your path. They may not look, act or think like you,

but God has placed them in your life for many reasons, including for you to shape them and for them to shape you. Jesus came to shift people's perspectives, especially on the issue of equality. He came to restore honor and dignity to those who were underserved and overlooked. Jesus died for all—male, female, black, brown, white. All ethnicities are afforded the same freedom in Christ.

I wish those deal leaders saw in me that which I can see. I was more than qualified to help land that deal, and I had earned my right to be on that team. But I was disqualified based on what I looked like. Jesus was also disqualified because of what he looked like. He was King but looked like an ordinary man. In fact, only his disciples and a few people who chose to open their eyes to who Jesus truly was knew the real Him. The Pharisees wanted to disqualify Him as not as powerful as He was. They were jealous of the influence He was having on His community and they wanted no part of it—as a matter of fact, they wanted to kill Him for it! Jesus did not give into conventional norms. He chose twelve of the most peculiar people to follow Him. Think about it—a tax collector, fishermen, a thief. These were not kings of the land. But God looked at the heart of these men. The love of his Father helped him to see past their sins, their betrayals, their positions in society.

My boss was able to do that too. When she cried with me and hugged me, I felt heard, supported, loved. She knew what it was like to be ostracized as a woman. She also felt helpless and powerless in trying to defend me joining on this trip. She understood the unfairness that is sometimes silent, and other times blatant. I was grateful to her then, and love the fact that we are still friends to this day. Sometimes we need not say a word, just stand and be still, as God is always working.

I never really connected the dots from that racial encounter in the 1980s to my life now until recently. I believe that sometimes when we face our hardest obstacles, we rise to the occasion at hand. That is, with the help of the Holy Spirit, and we must remember to ask for that help. Being left out of the deal team because of the color of my skin left an indelible mark on my life. Somehow, I knew from that day forward that it was my obligation to do whatever was in my power to help those who were underserved like me. I looked at my career as a place to help others, especially those who would have a tough time helping themselves.

I was raised in a family that did not see color, even though we were African Americans. My mom's grandmother was Irish, and she married an African American. Most of the men in our family at my generational level married outside the African American race. I was very accustomed to having family gatherings with mixed ethnic backgrounds; it was our normal. I will never forget my first two weeks in college, sitting at a lunch table with a group of young women I had just met. They were naming some of their male colleagues who were "hot," then would discuss whether the guy was Jewish or German or Irish. I innocently asked, "How do you know – did you ask them?"

A look of wide-eyed surprise came over the group. One young woman turned to me and said, "You're kidding, right? You do know you can usually tell someone's ethnicity by their last name!" I was embarrassed as this was not something discussed in my home. You did not guess at someone's ethnic background based on their last name, nor did you care.

As I moved along in my career, I found myself needing to do more for employees, the community, and my own family. I understood what it felt like to be left out, and wanted to go out of my way in whatever small fashion I could to help – especially women and people of color. As I became more advanced in my career, it gave me the opportunity to give back more, and to speak for the voiceless.

There are different ways to be an advocate for the voiceless. Some ways are on a smaller, more personal scale; others are larger and more strategic. Both are equally important. Around the year 2010, during a busy work day, I was briskly walking down a small hallway to get to my office. My boss, the division CEO, had an office next to mine. On my way, I first stopped at the office door of my boss, and noticed a young, well-dressed African American gentleman sitting in the chair facing the empty desk. He wore a dark blue business suit with matching tie, and a white crisp shirt. He was sitting tall with a football player-type physique.

"Hello, my name is Debra," I said with a smile. "Are you waiting for an interview?"

The gentleman immediately stood, turned to face me and extended his hand. "I know who you are," he stated with a grin. "I work here. As a matter of fact, I work in the same division as you!"

I was so embarrassed and upset with myself for assuming he was here for an interview. There were thousands of people in our division and I did not know every single one of them; however, since we had such a small percentage of African American men in our business, I thought I would have noticed him.

"My name is Jeffrey," he said. He was waiting to meet with our division CEO and I was curious as to what was going on. He then explained to me the dynamics. Jeffrey had attended a group meeting that my boss set up to speak with the junior staff. He was confident enough to respond to a question in this meeting that impressed my boss. Soon after the meeting, my boss asked the Human Resource representative to set up a meeting with Jeffrey.

"Wow, that's terrific. I'm so happy for you," I replied after hearing this story. After that first encounter, Jeffrey and I became fast friends. I watched him blossom into a more confident professional over the years. We would schedule meetings to catch up on business and life in general. I would ask him to think about the next steps of his career. The friendship grew and I was so honored when Jeffrey sent me an invitation to his wedding. Some time after that, baby pictures of his first son followed. When it was time for Jeffrey to move to another division within the company, I supported him with a glowing recommendation to the hiring manager.

Jeffrey taught me how one can help another on a personal, private, trusting level. It is such an honor to lift another as you climb. Jeffrey and I actually lifted each other. There are also broader-based, larger-scale ways to make a positive impact on someone's life. There is research and soul searching involved to be sure those opportunities are in the best interest of everyone involved. And the one lesson I learned along the way—pray on it first.

I remember my first seat on a nonprofit board. It was focused on women on Wall Street, and had been in existence since the early 1900s. The idea was to create a safe forum where women could gather to network, express ideas, challenge themselves and others, and broaden their depth and reach in financial services. The relationship began when the board directors met with our firm, including my senior sponsor at the time, to discuss the possibility of joining as a corporate member. This gave us the ability to involve more women across our firm, extend the ability for women at our firm to sit on a board, and give back to the New York-based community. I was thrilled when I was given an opportunity to become a director on this nonprofit board, as well as co-chair the events committee.

However, something more impactful happened with the partnering of this nonprofit board and my company. With our female senior executive vice president at the helm, a small group of women kicked off a women's initiative network at our company, leveraging the tools and capabilities of the nonprofit. I recall getting the invite from my sponsor for a breakfast meeting. I noticed on the invite that there were about ten or so other senior women invited. In her usual style, my sponsor whisked into the room with a big smile and said, "Hello, Ladies! Thanks for joining me this morning. It's time we do more for the women at our firm, and I need your help." From there it was history. Committees were formed, budgets created, events planned, feedback loops created, mentoring programs established—it just needed a few people to care (both men and women) and the rest fell into place. That initiative is still up and running today and is more impactful than ever. Another powerful gift, the women that founded that initiative are still connecting to this day. Most have retired and are focused on other life activities, however, the bond that was created several years ago is still going strong.

I stayed at my first board position for a few years, then the co-presidents approached me to consider becoming a co-president the following year. At the same time, a separate community-based nonprofit presented their mission to our firm, and wanted us to support their causes in the New York Metropolitan area. It was a long-standing organization, recognized nationally, known for helping women and children over several decades, mainly focused on daycare, girls' initiatives and afterschool programs. My sponsor asked me to spend some time getting to know them, so I started attending some of their events to get a better understanding of who they were and how they were helping the community. I was so impressed, I continued to show up to evening events, and began to personally donate to their cause.

Shortly thereafter, I received an email from the Program Director at this community-based nonprofit, requesting a lunch meeting. I asked a dear friend and colleague, Aniko, if she wanted to join me, as the nonprofit building was a short walk down Broadway from our offices, and a week or so later we went. The Program Director was an African American gentleman with dark curly hair, a medium build and a wide smile. He looked as though he worked out on a regular basis. He was with the Executive Director when we arrived, so we exchanged formal introductions and began a conversation about the state of nonprofits in New York City. The reliance of government funding was diminishing, which was causing concern for some traditional nonprofits. These organizations were looking to diversify their funding sources, and hence the original meeting with my company and ultimately me. The Program Director did not waste any time to get to the point. He asked if I would consider joining their board, which had about twenty-five directors at that time. I was shocked. I was already sitting on a smaller board and knew there was no way to handle two boards with my other responsibilities. I did not say yes or no at that meeting, but asked for some time to digest the request.

Soon after, I scheduled a call with my sponsor. We discussed our business goals and then moved into the community efforts. I mentioned being asked to be on the larger board, and how I felt I couldn't sit on two at once. I also told her that there was a potential to become a co-president on the smaller board. She asked me to be thoughtful in my consideration and to not just look at this opportunity from my lens, but to work to understand which organization can best help our company mission, and have community impact and sustainability. She also wanted me to get to know the other board members to understand if there is a wider networking net that would be cast broader in our organization and be mutually beneficial. I hung up the phone and was amazed by her insights, thoughts and guidance. I was so grateful to get her perspective.

I moved over to the larger new community-based board, and worked tirelessly for six years. My company was incredibly supportive and eventually became a corporate sponsor. At the end of my sixth year, the nonprofit Executive Director at that time ran into me coming out of my building on Wall Street one evening. She said, "This must be divine intervention—I was just thinking about you! As you know, our current board chair is stepping down. Will you consider becoming the board chair?" I accepted that board chair seat for another three years. It was challenging and yet one of the most rewarding assignments I have ever had. I was compelled to surrender the chair seat after the passing of my husband. In my heart I knew in this season, there was just somewhere else I had to be.

CHAPTER 4

Extended Relationships

I've felt a special bond with my extended family members since I was a young girl. There's something about our family that have caused even individuals outside it to comment on this blessing. It would take many years of maturity, experience and wisdom for me to recognize that we have a very special gift—deep, profound love. My Nana Grace and Papa Charlie demonstrated this to all of us on a regular basis. Of course, I had this indelible bond with my parents and siblings; but there was something more. My grandparents, aunts, uncles, nieces, nephews and cousins were one undivided nucleus. As a young girl, many Sundays were spent at Nana Grace and Papa Charlie's house in Maybrook, New York with the extended family.

My grandparents' house was a small, quaint bungalow-style home. Actually, my grandfather built the house after he and Nana got married. He was a hard worker and an excellent carpenter. Papa worked on the railroad while Nana took care of the house. During my childhood, their house did not seem small at all. The outside had reddish-black rustic asphalt siding with front and back porches. A screenhouse sat in the backyard, along with plenty of yard space to play and a big vegetable garden. Upon entering the front door, you stepped directly into the dining room. In the dining room there was a large wooden table with matching chairs and a china cabinet. We often gathered at that large table to share delicious homemade food. The living room was on the right side and was separated by wooden pillars. Nana kept her collection of saltshakers on top of those wooden pillars. Behind the living room was the master bedroom and a connecting smaller bedroom. A small narrow hallway off the dining area led to the bathroom, upstairs bedroom, kitchen and back mudroom. The house was always kept impeccably clean and smelled of comfort food or a breath of fresh air.

On these Sunday visits, Nana would cook a great meal of meat, vegetables and potatoes, and her older sister Aunt Bert would bring the big cardboard box filled with one of her famous yellow pound cakes. Nana would reach into her large freezer on the back porch and pull out the ice cream we had with every meal. My three siblings and I would be running around the house playing with our four cousins—Paul, Brent, Greg and Gerard. Life was grand! Nana exemplified how one holds tightly to their faith; Papa exemplified how one genuinely loves their family. The combination was astounding.

Throughout my life, my mom's sisters—Aunt Shirley, Aunt Grace and Aunt Mary—have been there as second mother figures. Always interested in my life, supporting me all the way, and providing gentle guidance when needed, even if they didn't necessarily agree with my choices. My mom and her siblings were remarkably close, and that in turn helped form the closeness I have with my two sisters, Tina and Susan, and my brother Frank, to this day. My siblings and I are so different yet so much alike. We grew up in a household filled with values, hard work and love.

My older sister, Tina, has always been my rock. When I had to plan the arrangements for my husband's funeral, she was there every step of the way. You see, she's always been there. When things are great, she's the one you want to call and hang out with because she's fun. And when the chips are down, she's the one who's going to assure you things are going to be okay. My younger sister, Sue, brings so much joy to the family. She has this *outrageous* sense of humor. One day when we were about 12 and 13 years old, we were laying on our beds in our shared bedroom daydreaming about the future. Sue told me she couldn't wait to have a "boyfriend" and then to marry him. She looked at me and said, "Do you want to get married one day?"

I hardly let her get the words out before saying, "Of course, no doubt!"

She then looked at me with those beautiful green eyes and said, "When I have a boyfriend, I'm going to practice absent!"

I said, "I think you mean abstinence!"

She didn't miss a beat. "No, silly, absent, 'cause I'm not going to be there for it to happen!" She started to giggle so hard she had tears running down her cheeks, and so did I. Sue and I have held onto that little joke for over forty-seven years. It's one of our little treasures.

My brother Frank takes after my dad, the provider. He actually looks like a carbon copy of my dad. He grew up in a house full of women, having three sisters, then getting married and ending up with another house full of women by having three daughters. He married Kim, my Irish sister-in-law, who I love dearly. Frank is a kind soul. Very protective, loves to see others enjoy their life, and will help out at the drop of a hat. I don't get to see my brother as much as I see my sisters due to his busy work schedule, but love him just the same.

The four of us are part of this indescribable fabric that our parents weaved together for us. We were four lucky kids; we knew we were loved. Our parents wanted a better life for us, and they worked hard to achieve it. Some of their few requests of us were to love one another, work hard, and care about other people. They truly lived the life of Christians and we were blessed to be their children. My parents' marriage was not perfect—they had their trials and tribulations—but they taught us how to withstand the wind, fight for what you believe in, and most of all ask God for help. They were married 60 years before my dad passed to Heaven. Before he did, my parents took over the tradition of Sunday gatherings. This time it was with their children, grandchildren and great-grandchildren.

Each Sunday we would arrive at my parents' home in Newburgh, New York with dish in one hand, beverage in the other. We would tell jokes, play games and share stories until late at night. It didn't matter that I had to get up at 5:30 the next morning to get ready for the commute to work. These Sunday gatherings were the heart and soul of our family.

In 1995, I was pregnant with my daughter Courtney. A routine test at the doctor came up positive for the possibility of a birth defect. My husband and I were distraught. My first call was to Aunt Shirley. She was the assistant director of nursing at a prestigious hospital in New York City, and I valued her guidance and views. Within twenty-four hours, Aunt Shirley came back with all the statistics of how the test could be incorrect, the options available to us, and a list of doctors for a second opinion. She was exceptional. My husband and I poured over the reports and asked her what felt like a hundred questions; she was respectful and had patience with us.

My husband and I finally just stopped. We looked at each other and my husband asked me, "What are we going to do if another doctor confirms a possible birth defect?"

I knew exactly where he was going with this question. I grew up with this man and our values were aligned. I turned and looked directly in his eyes and said what he was already thinking: "If God gives us a child with special needs, so be it. There's no decision for us to make here." We embraced, cried and called Aunt Shirley. I think she already knew the answer, but just allowed us to walk through the journey. We told her we were going to have this baby, so no more tests or special doctor visits were needed. She responded very calmly, "Yes, dear, I'm here if you need me." Through the grace of God, Courtney was born in 1996 as a healthy, happy baby girl.

As youngsters, without warning my dad would sometimes wake us up before the crack of dawn and say, "Let's go, grab some clothes, we're going to see Aunt Grace and Uncle George!" That was wonderful, but we were sound asleep, and they lived about 70 miles south in Flushing, New York. We would throw some clothes in a bag, stay in our pjs, and huddle in our station wagon as we headed to Flushing. As we kids slept in the back seat, Mom and Dad were in constant conversation in the front seat, laughing and reminiscing during the ride. When we arrived, we would run up to their front door and just start banging. Uncle George would rush down the stairs from their bedroom to see what all the commotion was about. Aunt Grace would be on his heels, peering from behind. They would let out a big, happy yelp when they saw us through the glass. Moments later, the dog was barking and my little cousins Greg and Gerard were wide awake.

We had successfully landed one of our famous "surprise visits" at Aunt Grace and Uncle George's house!

Before long, you could smell morning breakfast. Aunt Grace was in the kitchen firing up eggs, bacon, pancakes and home-fried potatoes. I never quite understood how she always had so much food in the house. They were so welcoming and loved when their family from upstate came to visit. This was our family. We could crash in on each other, ask for favors, just be there through thick and thin. For me, as a young girl, this was a very comforting feeling. I did not realize it was a special gift from God to be cherished forever. I know that now.

Aunt Mary has always been very special to me. She is a loving, faithful woman and a role model too. She and Uncle Bob provided my first job, babysitting for my cousins Paul and Brent. They trusted me at age 14 to watch their boys while they would grab some alone time. This babysitting job taught me how to negotiate, receive constructive criticism, and build fitness. Oh no, not from Aunt Mary and Uncle Bob—from my little cousins. You see, they had this big German Shepherd that was adorable but protective. Those little guys knew how to use that to their advantage. When it was time to come inside from playing, if they weren't ready, I heard "Duchess!" and here would come this eighty-pound dog running up to me as though to say, "Leave them alone!"

The fitness kicked in and I would run up to the deck for safety. Then my negotiation skills kicked in, and I promised the three of them treats if we all got back into the house in one piece. The constructive criticism came when I would spend the night and try to surprise the whole family by making pancakes in the morning. Well, sitting at the table in front of my aunt and uncle, my little cousin Brent blurted out, "These are burnt and taste horrible!" I took it in stride and over the years have worked on my cooking skills…somewhat.

As the years progressed, Aunt Mary would send kind notes with some pizza cash to me at college. "Just thinking of you, Deb" would be written on the card. The notes seemed to appear just at the right time. And when my life seemed to be at an all-time low point, God used Aunt Mary to gently guide me back to my faith. For that, I am eternally grateful.

Jesus had an even more profound idea of what it means to be family. He had to rely on his disciples to fulfill the role of family, since he knew Earth was not his true home and his real Father was His heavenly Father.

"While He was still speaking to the people, behold, his mother and his brothers stood outside, asking to speak to him. But he replied to the man who told him, 'Who is my mother, and who are my brothers?'

And stretching out his hand toward his disciples, he said, 'Here are my mother and my brothers! For whoever does the will of my Father in heaven is my brother and sister and mother.'" (Matthew 12:46-50, ESV)

"If anyone says, 'I love God,' and hates his brother, he is a liar; for he who does not love his brother whom he has seen cannot love God whom he has not seen. And this commandment we have from him: whoever loves God must also love his brother." (1 John 4:20-21, ESV)

We have to work hard to form deep, personal relationships, not only with immediate family members but with individuals God places in our lives. I have been blessed to have close friends who have become part of my extended family. It would be difficult to name everyone in that circle, but there are a few longstanding friends who have definitely shaped my life for the better.

In the late 1980s we had an awfully bad snow blizzard that hit the Hudson Valley. We lived in our first home in Marlboro at the time; Harry worked the night shift, so he had already left for work. I was settling in for the evening when I heard a knock on the door. I wasn't expecting company and it was unusual to have a visitor at this late hour. I thought perhaps my neighbors, Rick and Dori, might be in trouble. They were an older Italian couple and the nicest neighbors.

I ran to the corner of the picture window and peeked outside to see who was at the door. There stood a fair-skinned African American woman, about 5'8", bundled in a heavy coat, scarf and boots. I thought, *Who is this?* I went to the door and opened it enough to speak to her. She started to speak with a big smile and beautiful white teeth, saying, "Hey, it's Gail! We met at the shopping center last summer with Lewis and Harry, remember?" Yes, of course I remembered Gail. Lewis had been a family friend since I could remember. He grew up in the city area with my husband. He's a great guy.

The snow and ice were falling heavily at this point. Gail was standing on the covered porch, visibly cold as she was speaking. I hurriedly asked her to come in. "I'm so sorry to bother you at this time in the evening, but I'm terrified to drive in this weather. Can I stay here for a bit?" she asked.

Without hesitation I replied, "Of course you can!" We were able to talk and really get to know each other into the wee hours of the night. We had a small spare bedroom in the house that worked out fine for Gail. She slept over and headed out in the morning, after the plows were able to clear up the roads. The miracle of all this is that Gail and I are great friends today, and are still sharing life together. She and Lewis have been there through our marriage, the birth of our children, joining us on vacations and holidays, and sharing in our grief in times of despair. They are not merely friends; they are part of the sacred blessing of relationships that God provides to all of us. We in turn have to recognize, be thankful for, and understand that this is a true gift, never to be taken for granted.

I started my four-hour-plus daily commute to work from the Hudson Valley to New York City in 1982. I remember at that time thinking, *This is too much. I'll do it just for a little while.* Well, almost thirty-five years later, upon retirement I finally stopped that commute. But something magical happened on it. In 1984, I was trying to find a seat one morning. As sad as it is to admit, there was a bit of prejudice that I tried to avoid during this era as it related to seat selection on the commuter train. I silently observed that if you were a person of color, generally you were the last person to get a seatmate as nobody wanted to sit next to you. However, when the train was packed and all that was left were the middle seats, you were the first to be interrupted for someone to squeeze into that middle seat. It's an observation I watched in silence, disbelief and anger for many years.

On this particular morning, I sat next to this well-dressed Italian woman with shiny black hair and a small frame. I had briefly met this woman previously through a mutual friend. She was eating her breakfast sandwich out of a foil wrap. I said "excuse me" and sat down. We exchanged pleasantries and small talk ensued. "I'm so impressed you have time to fix breakfast in the morning—it smells good," I chuckled.

She responded by saying, "Oh, if it weren't for my husband's grandfather, I'd starve! He makes me a sandwich for work each morning."

Wow, I was beyond impressed. *Now that's a granddad,* I thought to myself. We started to talk about our jobs and what we did for a living. We were both tied to the financial services side of the business; she on the broker/trading side, me on the product/servicing side. We were so young, just starting out on our careers, and had similarly high hopes and aspirations for great things in life. Natalie was married with no children when we met. I had my long-standing boyfriend. Just two gals trying to live our best life. I remember when Natalie was pregnant with her son, Grant. Her water broke early, which caused her to be hospitalized. The doctors were trying to prevent her from going into labor as she still had a way to go until full term. Her family came to visit her in the hospital from Staten Island. I had met some of them over the years and they are a big, loving family. I remember walking into the hospital room and thinking, *Great, she's sitting up in the chair.* No, it was her sister! That's how much they resembled one another to me.

I walked next to her bed and she greeted me with arms outstretched. "Debbie, I can't believe you came! How sweet of you!" She was smiling and seemed comfortable in the bed. I was torn during this visit, as I wasn't exactly sure what I would say to her. The doctors had told her there was clear and present danger in her situation, but Natalie never mentioned the situation during that visit. She spoke to me about what she had bought to prepare for the baby's homecoming; the diaper genie, the diapers, the non-alcoholic wipes and much more. It felt like I was visiting someone who had been admitted into the hospital to have their baby on a regular schedule. After my visit, I kissed Natalie and her family goodbye and walked out of the room totally stunned.

Grant was born premature, and is a happy, healthy young man today. Years later I asked Natalie how she had the courage to stay so strong, so optimistic? She replied, "What other choice did I have?" It was a moving lesson I learned from my dear friend, and one I would use over and over again in my own life. Natalie and I are still great friends to this day and have shared life's blessings and challenges. We are not on that daily commuter train anymore, but our tracks are still connected.

CHAPTER 5

Recognizing Grace

Grace is a true gift from God. There have been many instances in my life that have turned out as a true positive blessing when I expected them to turn out negatively, whether large-scale life-changing events or small, hardly noticeable ones. Once when my daughter Courtney was 1 ½ years old, as usual she was playing with big brother Harry, who was almost 4 ½ years older. Both my husband and I were at home, and all four of us had a lovely dinner at the dining table, thanks to my husband being a great cook. After dinner, my husband retreated downstairs to his man cave, and I began to clear the table and scrape the dishes while the kids were playing with one another in the hallway. Courtney loved following her big brother around the house, and we were pleased as parents that they had such a loving relationship. Harry was just as pleased to have his little sister so interested in what he was doing.

It seemed as though I had only turned my head for a second before I heard a loud shriek from my daughter. I will never get that sound out of my head. As I turned to see what happened, I noticed the bathroom door closed, and my daughter's tiny right-hand fingers stuck within the closed door jam. I began to scream, "Oh no, help, please help!" My husband was next to me in two seconds flat as he had heard Courtney's scream too.

I opened the door to release her fingers and noticed the wide-eyed look on my son's face. He had just been trying to go to the bathroom and his sister followed him in. Blood was everywhere. Courtney was screaming at the top of her lungs. Then her brother began to cry and scream too when he saw all the blood.

And then it happened. I looked at Courtney's hand. There, next to her pinky, her index finger had been severed. The tip was completely gone. I started to shout to my husband, "Her finger is missing! Oh my God, her finger is missing!" My husband didn't wait for 911; he grabbed a towel, wrapped Courtney's bloody hand, and said, "Get Harry and get in the car!"

The next few minutes were an out-of-body experience. I ran to the bathroom and got down on my hands and knees, moving my hands across the floor until I felt a soft piece of flesh, which was the tip of my daughter's finger! I ran to the kitchen as Harry was putting on the kids' coats and holding them both tightly. I grabbed a small yellow plastic bowl then went to the freezer for ice. I threw the tip of the finger and the ice in that bowl and ran out to the car to meet my family.

The drive to the hospital felt like forever. Courtney was screaming, as was our son Harry. Horrible things were going through my head. We had both been at home, within two feet of our children. *How could this happen?* Harry sped to the hospital, through red lights and stop signs, actually hoping we would get the attention of a police officer to escort us. No such luck. We arrived frantically at the emergency room with Courtney screaming in my husband's arms, and my hand gripping our son's hand as to not lose him. I shouted to the security guard and the registration personnel, "Help us! Her finger! Her finger, please!" We were rapidly whisked away to the back room, as someone approached us to get basic information about our insurance and how this incident occurred.

They quickly gave Courtney a numbing shot to alleviate some of her pain. I was so relieved, and she seemed to calm a bit after. A nurse approached me with brownish blond hair. She seemed to be about 35 years old, medium build and about 5'7". She wore the typical white nurse outfit and spoke in a lighthearted, kind voice. She saw that we were beyond distraught and approached us gingerly. After she introduced herself, she wanted us to know that everything would be okay, and after looking at Courtney's finger the doctor agreed they would stitch it up across the top and we would be all set.

I couldn't say much, but I managed to say, "What are you talking about? Are you trying to tell us she lost the top of her finger forever? I gave you her finger—can't you reattach it?" I began to sob uncontrollably. My husband grabbed my son and left the room, as he didn't want our son to see me in that state. He had already seen enough that evening. The nurse began to explain how difficult it is to successfully reattach a finger, unfortunately making light of it at a very inappropriate time by stating, "Perhaps she'll just get a nail extension for that finger when she grows up and it won't be that noticeable."

I continued to cry. "I don't understand how you can spend the time to care and love so deeply for your children, and in an instant such bad things happen," I gulped between breaths. This is when it happened again, another out-of-body experience. Words were coming out of my mouth, however I had no understanding of how I even knew what to say next. "Is there a hand surgeon in the hospital?" I heard the words pouring out of my mouth.

"Well, there's Dr. B on call, but it would take time for him to get here. Besides, that solution would be rather expensive."

"You call the doctor, I'll worry about the costs," I said, perhaps a bit chillier than intended. Within thirty minutes Dr. B arrived and was looking at Courtney's damaged finger and the little yellow bowl with the ice and tip. My husband and son had returned to the room by this time. The hand surgeon pulled us aside and said, "I can try to reattach, but there's no guarantees here. It's up to you if you want to take the chance and consider this treatment."

My husband and I didn't need to think twice. We replied at the same time, "Please, do what you can."

Courtney's finger was reattached that evening in the emergency room. She was fitted for a cast on her right hand to keep the movement still, and a sling to rest her arm. It broke our hearts to see our little girl who should be laughing and playing all bandaged up this way. I remember feeling very isolated when this incident happened. My extended family was there for us; however, it felt as though they just didn't know what to say or do.

After a few weeks of healing, we went into Dr. B's office for the first visit of many. This would be the first time we would see the finger since the night in the emergency room. Dr. B gently removed the bandages from Courtney's finger. I closed my eyes and took a deep breath. When I opened my eyes, I felt dizzy. I grabbed my husband's arm for fear of falling. Courtney's finger was completely black and very thin. It did not look like a finger at all. I thought, *Oh no, the procedure didn't work.* Tears began to well up in my eyes just as Dr. B turned to look at me and my husband. "It looks good, healing nicely!" Dr. B said with a smile. "Will see you in a few weeks. Keep it dry," he added. I couldn't believe the words I was hearing! The finger looked awful to me. I was not going to question his opinion and quickly swooped our daughter up and headed for the door.

After several months, Courtney's finger completely healed, and she doesn't remember the incident at all. Her brother barely remembers it as well. Over the years I have chosen not to recall that frightful night, and it is hard writing it in this book. I have a much different perspective of that incident now. I understand it was the Holy Spirit that gave me the strength to get down on the floor to look for Courtney's finger. He also put the words in my mouth to ask about a hand surgeon. It was God's saving grace to use Dr. B that evening to give us hope.

Sometimes bad things happen, and we focus on the terrifying moment that takes our breath away. I had to learn to take a pause and ask God for help. He always answers.

It was a warm day in April 1975 when I arrived home from junior high school. As soon as I hit the front door, I knew something was wrong. There was a silence in the house that was unusual for that time of day. My father's car was parked in the driveway, so he was home. *It was too early for him to be home from work, though,* I thought. As I made my way through the living room to the kitchen, the lights were on but nobody was there. *Strange,* I thought. I slowly walked down the narrow hallway towards my parents' bedroom. I could see their bedroom door slightly cracked open. I peeked inside to see my parents fully clothed, laying on the bed. At first I thought they were napping, which was usual for my dad but not for my mom. But after 20 seconds I realized they weren't sleeping, but were embraced and weeping.

I turned away from their door and ran back through the living room, up the stairs to our bedrooms to find one of my siblings. As I hit the top step, I heard a whimper coming from my oldest sister Tina's room. I threw open her door and yelled, "What's going on? Why is everyone so upset?"

Tina raised her head from the pillow, looked at me through tear-stained eyes, and said matter-of-factly, "I'm pregnant." She was eighteen years old and about to graduate from high school in a couple of months.

I felt the floor fall from beneath my legs. I knew it had to be a ridiculous nightmare, and I would soon wake up. My stomach automatically started to ache. I started to cry with my sister. "I don't understand. Are you sure?" I managed to ask her.

"Yes, I'm almost six months along," my sister shared. *How is this possible?* I thought. We all noticed she was gaining weight, but not to the extent that she was carrying a baby. I remember attending one of my sister's basketball games during this time. My dad helped to coach the games, and Tina was one of the best players. She had always been so active and fit. She was a cheerleader in high school, and very popular based on her beauty and charm. I felt lucky to be her sister. During this particular game, Tina went up for a shot and her basketball shirt raised a little to expose her belly. I then heard my dad lean over to the other coach and jokingly comment, "My Tina's getting a little beer belly – she needs to watch it!" That scene flashed before my eyes when my sister said she was pregnant.

This news was shocking for my sister, my family and our small-town community. We were a middle-class Catholic family that felt there were no limits in life as long as you had your faith, family, hard work and integrity.

We grew up as a very close-knit extended family, so this wasn't just my sister's circumstance—this had an impact across our entire family.

It was hard to see our family go through this and try to have a brave face. My sister was of course devastated, as the man who got her pregnant denied it was him. They had been dating for a couple of years and he virtually disappeared after this happened. The decision for my sister to have and raise this baby was never up for discussion. Adoption was out of the question as my parents could not fathom having a grandchild they would never see. I had a hard time trying to understand it all. My parents were so upset and, although they had four children, there was one who desperately needed their full attention. I began to feel as though I did not want to ride the bus, go to school or see anyone, for fear of them questioning me about my sister. I became very anxious and it began to feel as though I was the one pregnant.

I physically, mentally and emotionally could not take the stress anymore. I regretted coming home to a house filled with sadness and sometimes anger. My sister eventually went to live with my mom's sister in Flushing, New York to deliver the baby. I think it was easier on my parents and the doctors were particularly good there. I continued to feel depressed and sad. I walked into my bedroom one afternoon and shut the door behind me. I fell down on my knees and sobbed. I asked God to take this burden away from me. I begged to feel better, as I was lost. I asked Him, how does this happen to good families?

I confessed I could hardly bear it. It was quiet in that room. And then almost instantaneously, I dried my tears and stood up from the floor, opened the door and walked downstairs. My heart felt light and the feeling of gloom was gone. In my head I heard the words, *You are not the pregnant one. You will all get through this.* And we did.

Gina was born in the summer of 1975. My dad pulled in the driveway with my sister and this new, beautiful baby in the back seat. It was a hot July day. My sister looked tired but good. I ran down the sidewalk and grabbed the baby out of my sister's arms. I looked at Gina's wavy black hair, button nose and beautiful brown face, and knew all was well with the world. What I couldn't have imagined that day is that the little girl I was holding in my arms would be the one to save my husband's life forty-three years later. She gave him a gift that can never be repaid. God used her to allow my husband to fully embrace his faith and our Savior, two weeks before he went to Heaven.

"When they had finished breakfast, Jesus said to Simon Peter, 'Simon son of John, do you love me more than these?' He said to him, 'Yes, Lord; you know that I love you.' He said to him, 'Feed my lambs.' He said to him a second time, 'Simon son of John, do you love me?' He said to him, 'Yes, Lord, you know that I love you.' He said to him, 'Tend my sheep.' He said to him the third time, 'Simon son of John, do you love me?' Peter was grieved because he said to him the third time, 'Do you love me?' And he

*said to him, 'Lord, you know everything; you know
that I love you.' Jesus said to him, 'Feed my sheep.'"
(John 21:15-17, ESV)*

This passage is perhaps one of the most blatant
examples of the extent of God's grace towards his children,
Peter's reinstatement into the family of God. What did
Peter do before this exchange with Jesus? Denied him.
Even after Jesus predicted Peter would deny him three
times, Peter didn't believe it. That is, until the rooster
crowed after the third time and Jesus looked him right
in the eye. Humiliated and wracked with guilt, it looked
as though Peter could never undo his awful denial.
Yet Jesus, as an extension of God's grace, gives him an
opportunity to return, and to pay forward the love he
received from Jesus by loving God's people and feeding
them with His Word.

I felt so guilty when I saw my daughter's finger in that
door jam. As a mother, there's nothing I wouldn't do to
protect my child. Stricken with fear and overcome with
guilt, I thought her finger was beyond repair. Yet God in
His grace chose to use the talents of others to restore her
finger. In the same way, my sister's willingness to have a
baby from a father who denied her took great courage.
God, again in his grace, chose to use her daughter to not
only change my sister's life, but the same baby we could
have easily given away was used to save my husband's life.
I look at my sister's life now, so blessed with children and

grandchildren. They fill her life, and my brother-in-law David's life, with so much love, joy and hope.

Often we take grace for granted. But when we choose to recognize it, it is proof positive we serve a Savior who cares more about transforming us to His likeness than he does in punishing us for our behaviors. He truly is our Redeemer.

CHAPTER 6

The Blue Bird

At 40 years old, I felt this deep, nagging pain in my belly. I have dealt with this pain for several months now, never mentioning it to anyone, including my husband. One cold, dark evening, I'm laying on the couch in our living room groaning in pain. I break out in a deep sweat. I sprint about ten feet to open the front door. I feel the cold rush of wind as the door opens. Panting, I struggle to breathe. The feeling of a cold wet towel over my forehead has cured many ailments for me in the past, so I shout, "Compress, compress!" My husband comes running up the stairs from his man cave. Usually, the compress stress signal means I've had one too many glasses of wine and didn't feel well. Not this evening. Harry takes one look at me and says, "I think you need to go to the hospital." No arguments here.

"I think you're going to leave here without a gallbladder," the tall, dark-haired doctor states matter-of-factly. I find myself laying in a hospital bed surrounded by two strange men peering over my body. The room smells like tin, and the sterility is unnerving. The taller doctor starts again, "We're happy you came in. Your enzyme levels are extremely high." The doctors begin to discuss a procedure they'll need to do soon, where they will lubricate my throat and insert a camera to look at my stomach area.

"Will it hurt?" I quiver.

"Nah, not that bad," the shorter doctor responds. They leave the room abruptly and I realize I'm all alone at this hospital, in this room, in this bed. It was a late night in the emergency room and took quite some time to get clearance for a bed. *Harry must be home dealing with the children and will come back later. I hope.*

I feel this sense of despair starting to well inside me. I'm about to start guiltily feeling sorry for myself when a head pops around the opening door. "Hey there. I heard you were here. How do you feel?" It's my second cousin, George's long-time girlfriend Ruth! I don't see them often and I was beyond surprised to see her in my hospital room.

"What on Earth are you doing here?" I ask. Ruth replies that she's here to see me. We catch up on family happenings and then she asks what the next step is. I explain that I'll need a procedure at any moment to see how bad things are, but most likely the gallbladder will need to be removed.

Minutes later a nurse comes in and notifies me that I need to go down for the procedure and will be back in about an hour. Ruth looks at me and says, "I'll be here when you get back. Everything is going to be fine." I tell her that's not necessary and thank her for the visit. The procedure is done as described, and I'm wheeled back to my room. As the gurney turns the corner into my room, I notice feet in a chair on the far side. *It must be Harry,* I think. To my surprise, it's Ruth. She stayed and waited for the procedure to be over. She walks over to the bed once I'm settled back into it and says, "How did it go?"

I was awake for the procedure, so I shared with her my feelings of being a little afraid but all in all not that bad. "That's great," she says, then hands me a tiny glass blue bird. "I saw this in the gift shop and thought it might lift your spirits," Ruth states. My eyes begin to swell with tears. The visit is enough, and now this beautiful gift is more than I can handle. "What's the matter?" she asks.

I grab her hand and say, "Nothing, nothing at all. I can never thank you enough for this."

Ruth doesn't know the joy that blue bird still gives me every time I look at it. It sits in my bedroom on top of my jewelry holder. It's been there for more than twenty years. For me, it represents the highest act of kindness. Ruth didn't know me very well. She gave me her precious time and a lasting gift, not a physical gift but a spiritual one. The blue bird is a reminder to me to act like Ruth. Be kind and generous with your time. Not only to your family and friends, but to those you may not see that often.

I said thank you to Ruth in that hospital room. I'm not sure that was enough. Thank you for making me a better person, for teaching me unselfish giving and pure kindness.

"And let us not grow weary of doing good, for in due season we will reap, if we do not give up. So then, as we have opportunity, let us do good to everyone, and especially to those who are of the household of faith." (Galatians 6:9-10, ESV)

Chapter 7

God's Will

There have been events in my life and in the world in general that cause confusion, sadness and misunderstanding. Over the years, I've come to learn that there are things in this world that no human being is capable of stopping, solving or overcoming. Some things are of a higher power than any of us. As we try to understand what's happening, this is when almighty faith must prevail. Not all things will be revealed to us, not all questions will be answered, and not all days will be filled with joy.

It was a beautiful fall morning in September 2001. I exited the subway station outside my building on Wall Street and headed through the heavy entry doors. I made a quick left turn after the security entrance to reach the elevators to head to the 39th floor. As I entered the elevator, a woman with wavy dark hair, glasses, and a thick build came running through the elevator doors, hysterical. "My friend, my friend, she's in that building, I know she's hurt, oh no..." she sobbed uncontrollably.

The elevator doors shut. I looked at her and calmly said, "I'm sure your friend is okay. It's all going to be okay. What happened?"

She looked at me with red, wet eyes and said, "A plane, it went into the building at the World Trade Center!" By this time, the elevator doors opened to her floor and off she went as quickly as she had come. I continued the journey up to the 39th floor and stepped off the elevator.

I entered our office space where our small team was huddled at the windows. One of my colleagues shouted to me, "Debra, you're not going to believe this – as clear as it is outside, a plane ran into a building!" I threw my belongings down and raced to the window. I wasn't prepared to see what came next. Due to the extreme heat caused by that plane, people were jumping out of the high towers immediately to save their lives. And we were the witnesses to this. My stomach began to ache and just as we thought it couldn't get any worse…a second plane slammed into the building. My colleague shouted, "Let's go!" Within moments our building security alarms were ringing, and over the P.A. system we were being instructed to proceed to the ground floor via the stairwells. One of my colleagues on this small team had multiple sclerosis. She was a young woman, full of energy and a zest for life. I took on a personal mission to stay with her to see that she got on her way.

The news was starting to trickle in that this was a planned terrorist attack, although at that time we didn't understand how widespread. My young colleague and

I locked eyes, and we could see that we both just wanted to get down to the ground floor and the subway station. She lived uptown, and I had to go uptown to catch a train from Grand Central to get home. Eventually, we made our way downstairs to the lobby level where the chaos continued. By this time the first tower had unexpectedly begun to fall, and there were folks taking cover on the lowest floors of our building. My colleague and I waited in the line to exit the building. We pushed the revolving doors to exit and on the streets of downtown Manhattan there were people running in all directions. The sirens were loud, a white ash filled the air, and the stench of smoke and fire was everywhere. I silently prayed to God, *Please not now, not like this.* We ran down the subway steps that were right outside our building. Shortly thereafter, an uptown train entered the station. We jumped on and grabbed a seat. We looked at each other in amazement. At this time in the morning, the train wasn't that busy; the riders were calmly listening to music, a young lady was reading her magazine, a mother was whispering to her children to play nice. The beat of the subway was very usual for unusual circumstances. Then it dawned on me. I leaned over to my colleague and whispered, "Oh my goodness, they don't even know what's happening above us." We sat in silence until the announcement came for Grand Central Station and I hugged my colleague and jumped off the train.

As I made my way up the stairs to the main area, the announcements were hurried and frequent. People were hustling about to find out information. At that moment I realized that I should call home to let my family know I was okay. I dug around in my bag and grabbed my cell phone. I selected the number labeling "home" and waited. As I continued to wait for a connection, I noticed many of us trying to do the same thing. We had flooded the signals, and it was very difficult to connect a line. Finally, I heard ringing and my husband picked up by calling my name: "Deb? Is that you, Deb? Are you okay?" I assured him I was fine and would be on the next train out of Grand Central. I told him they were running extra trains to get folks out of the City as quickly as possible.

Then panic set in. "Where are the kids?" I heard my voice quiver. Harry replied with a strong voice, "The kids are fine. Harry's on his way home and Courtney's afternoon kindergarten was cancelled. The schools are closing early, and Harry should be home on the bus any minute now." I then asked my husband how widespread this attack was and if they were in any danger. He said not to worry, that they were safe, and he just wanted me to get home as soon as possible. I hung up the phone and ran over to the large schedule screen to decipher when the next train would be heading upstate. I had ten minutes to get to the track. As I walked down the plank towards the waiting train, I was surrounded by a sea of worried and frightened commuters.

The train was packed so I made my way towards the back where there were still a few seats left. Not long after I sat down, we began to pull away from the station, heading out of the tunnel. "We're all going to die, I tell you! We're going to die!" a middle-aged woman shouted at the top of her lungs. An older man replied, "Shut up, don't say that! Sit down and just be quiet!"

I bent my head towards my knees and laid my head in my hands. *What is happening,* I thought. We felt so helpless—and worse yet, hopeless. As we were riding on the train, more devastating news. The second tower fell. There were more shouts and cries and moans from some of the riders. I was numb at this point, in a state of shock and disbelief. I started to think of all those people who had woken up this morning just to go to work, and wouldn't ever come home again.

I felt deep grief during September 11th. I'm not sure I even knew what it was at that time. We lost nearly 3,000 souls on that dreadful day. John G. was one of them. John was a firefighter who lived in the Hudson Valley and worked in New York City. His wife, Roxanne, was the owner of my children's daycare center. John was a quiet, friendly guy. He was forty-seven years old when he passed to Heaven. He had a love for music and environmental science. He was a great dad with two sons and a daughter. Often when I would ride past the daycare center, I would see him working on the lawn or hauling materials for his wife. John, like many other firefighters, responded to the burning towers that day and sacrificed his life. I will never forget him. I've placed my hand on his name at the Freedom Tower memorial site, found his picture at the 911 Memorial Museum, and together with my children recently found his name at the memorial site at the Arboretum here in the Hudson Valley. I didn't get to say this to him but I must say it now: *Thank you, John.*

Eventually we all returned to work, school and play; but the world, especially New York City, was forever changed. And so was I.

How much more grief could I handle after September 11th? I've learned that there's my will and there's almighty God's will. In March 2009, for example, I awoke to a light windy day with green grass, budding trees and dark gray clouds. It felt like any other weekend morning to me. I cleared the breakfast dishes and was beginning to start my day when the phone rang. Unexpectedly it was Aunt Shirley, mentioning that she was at the hospital in New York City with my Uncle Artie. He'd been in and out of the hospital of late, a lung cancer survivor after having major surgery several years earlier. "Hello, honey," she stated in a curt, exasperated tone. "I thought I'd call, as Uncle Artie isn't really feeling well today. I'm here at the hospital with him."

I responded immediately by telling her I would come down to the City and be with both of them. She insisted it wasn't necessary, that she had only reached out to let other members of the family know her whereabouts in case we were looking for her. I hung up. An uncomfortable feeling came over me. Aunt Shirley usually doesn't call early in the morning. I heard a sense of panic in her voice even though she was guarding it. I reached for the phone to call my sister, Tina. "I just got a call from Aunt

Shirley about Uncle Artie," I blurted. "I don't know why, but I think we need to go down there – now!" Tina and I then reached out to my mom and my niece Jessica, and away we went to New York City. I offered to drive all of us down, and the 60-mile drive felt like 600 miles.

Uncle Artie's nieces and nephews didn't get to see him often, as he lived further away and was dealing with his health issues. He and Aunt Shirley never had children… they had all of us! I remember one summer job working in New York City as an intern at Aunt Shirley's hospital, while I was also living with them in Queens. What a great summer for a young gal. To travel to work, I had to walk a few blocks from their home to the bus station, and Uncle Artie would peer from the eighth-floor terrace making sure I was okay. I never told him I saw him watching over me, but he always did. He loved his music and made tapes for my then future husband. He would label the tapes and have Aunt Shirley mail them or bring them upstate on her next visit. Uncle Artie so enjoyed listening to the smooth sounds of rhythm and blues. Before he became ill, he was also a barber and found joy in his work. When our son HJ turned one year old, he gave him his first haircut at my grandmother's house, lifting him into a chair stacked with pillows. Tears formed in HJ's big brown eyes and he began to reach for his dad. In his deep "Barry White" voice, Uncle Artie gently said, "It's okay, little man, this'll be over before you know it!" For whatever reason, HJ calmed down and the haircut was successful. I still have those locks from HJ's first haircut in my hope chest.

In the car on the way to the hospital my thoughts were jumbled. *When were we going to get there?* I pictured Aunt Shirley asking the doctors a ton of questions, given her nursing background, while still tending to Uncle Artie. I didn't want Uncle Artie to be in pain. They usually checked his vitals and were able to give him some medication to help with his pain. *We can sit with Uncle Artie while Aunt Shirley grabs some food*, I thought. *Knowing her, she probably rushed to the hospital on an empty stomach. Please traffic, move faster.*

Just then I heard a cell phone ring in the backseat. I then overheard, "Yes. Well, we're actually on our way and should be there very soon." The conversation ended quickly. The voice in the back seat whispered to the rest of us, "He just passed."

In March 2014, the whole family turned up for a party for my first-born nephew, Russell, an incredibly talented singer (rapper). The center was decorated with colorful tables, and as usual the food was flowing. The purpose of this gathering was to promote a music CD Russell had created. There was dancing, performances, great conversation, tasty beverages and delicious food. My sister Sue's fingerprints were all over it, as she's the ultimate party planner. It was good fun. My Uncle Bob and Aunt Mary were there among forty or so other guests. Uncle Bob has always been the cool uncle. He dresses well, speaks well, and parties well. He has a love for his family that goes very deep. As a young girl, I admired the playful relationship between him and Aunt Mary. I remember one beautiful summer day at my parents' house, we were preparing for a family barbeque and Aunt Mary and Uncle Bob had come early to help set up. I was probably in junior high school at the time. We were setting up tables and at one point Uncle Bob started to horseplay with Aunt Mary. She started to giggle and say, "Bob, stop that right now, Deb is watching!" Well, my head whipped around to see what was going on, and they were both tickling each other, giggling like teenagers and having their own little party over there. I remember smiling to myself and hoping Harry and I would one day have that type of excitement at that age if we ever got married.

At Russell's party this particular evening, Uncle Bob was wearing a pair of pressed jeans, a collared shirt and a vest. He seemed a little out of sorts—not as talkative as usual, lethargic, frequenting the men's room multiple times. Later I found out he was venturing to the men's room to get warm, as he was freezing in the main room. A few days later, Aunt Mary confides that he was coughing and on bedrest. She continued encouraging him to see a doctor, which he did. A bunch of tests were run and at first the doctors thought it might be some sort of respiratory issue, so they guarded against visitation. But I was scheduled to leave on a business trip at this time, and the thought of leaving without seeing Uncle Bob was unbearable. Against orders, I showed up on his hospital floor. The nurse gave me a mask to wear as I entered his room. He grinned when he saw me. "What are you doing here?" were his first words to me.

"I couldn't stay away – sorry. I'm leaving for a business trip and wanted to see you before I left," I gingerly responded.

A few minutes later his cell phone rang, and he told Aunt Mary I was there visiting. He hung up the phone and then turned to me. "How are the kids?" he asked. I told him they were great and miss him. I asked him how he was feeling. "I feel okay, it's just this thing in my chest…they want to do more tests," he responded, rubbing his chest with no eye contact. After about 15 minutes, the nurse came into the room to administer his daily medications. I kissed Uncle Bob on the forehead and told him I loved him.

It wasn't long after that business trip when the doctors diagnosed Uncle Bob with late-stage lung cancer. That September, as he was battling cancer, he planned a wonderful surprise birthday party for Aunt Mary, and invited the entire family to celebrate. We all had such a wonderful time. I walked over to Uncle Bob's table to see how he was doing. He had a serious look on his face and said, "Please take a picture with my wife, her sisters and me. Can you go get them now?" I jumped up immediately and gathered everyone for the picture. We placed Uncle Bob in the middle of his wife and sisters-in-law. At first, I thought Uncle Bob wanted that snapshot for himself. Not at all; he left that picture as a gift to them. A wonderful reminder that no matter what, they will always be together. They will always be family.

There's a song that played at that party and every time I hear it, I know Uncle Bob is right here. He taught me many things I will never forget: when greeting your spouse hold your kiss for at least ten seconds; that it's okay to nurture yet lovingly discipline your children; to set aside time for acts of kindness; and to never forget to keep your faith and family first, no compromises. I miss my Uncle Bob. But somehow God has let me hold on to the best part of him.

⌒

One Sunday in December 2015, it was just another one of our lively visits at my mom and dad's house. It was the regular crew, consisting of my parents, siblings, nieces and nephews. As usual the food and beverages were flowing, and the noise decibel was at fever pitch. It was time to fill each other in on what had transpired in the previous week, and the big events coming up at work, in school or during life in general. The elders sat at the kitchen table and the younger generation spilled into the sitting room down the hall. Mom and Dad seemed to be in a particularly good mood. They loved when their children and grandchildren visited, and shared a meal and some good stories with them. All our kids had such a wonderful relationship with their grandparents. A true treasure.

Dad had been on oxygen for several months and was visiting doctors to find out what was the main cause for his shortness of breath. He was still his jolly self and tried to keep up on his daily routines as much as possible. He had fully retired more than ten years ago, and said it was one of the best decisions he ever made. When I was young, I couldn't picture my dad "retired." He was the energizer bunny that kept going and going. He was a great role model for what a true work ethic should look like.

As we were sitting at the kitchen table, I noticed my dad looking particularly good this evening. He was wearing a dark turtleneck shirt and a pair of casual pants. He always wore his cross that was brightly shining against the dark colored shirt. We were so accustomed to him romping around in his pajamas, so it was a treat to see him fully dressed. His smile was bright, and his skin seemed to glow with a hue of restfulness. He threw his head back in laughter and added his funny side comments to enhance whatever was being discussed. He was totally enjoying himself.

The night seemed to fly by in a flash, and soon it was time to clean up and head home. After clearing up the dishes from the kitchen table, I hugged and kissed Mom goodnight. I walked down the hall to the sitting room, as Dad had moved there to sit in his comfy recliner. The TV was playing in the background as I walked towards his chair. "Okay, Dad, we've got to go home," I said, looking into his eyes before I kissed him goodnight. "I love you, Dad."

He held me tight and said, "I love you too, honey. Be good."

My commute to work the next morning was pretty typical. I made a mental note to buy a new pair of stockings on the way in. I reached for my cell phone to catch up on emails. I got stuck on one email from a relationship manager (RM) about offering a product our team produces to a specific client. The RM and I were going back and forth on the issue. My phone then rang – it was my sister, Tina. "Hey, sorry to bother you," she stated in a calm voice, "but wanted to let you know Dad was rushed to the hospital this morning. Mom just called and said she had to call the ambulance as he had a breathing attack."

"Is Mom with him?" I asked.

"No, they wouldn't let her ride in the ambulance. But Michael's on his way down to the hospital." My nephew Michael is such a loving, caring person. As I'm writing this, he's in his mid-twenties and serving our country in the Middle East.

I quickly disconnected from Tina and called Mom at her home. "Hi Mom. What happened?" I anxiously inquired.

Mom was panting heavily as I tried to listen and digest what she was telling me. "They came and took him. Dad got up to go to the bathroom. I heard him struggling. When I arrived at the bathroom door he was on the floor. He couldn't breathe. I called 911. They helped me go through CPR on the phone. Oh, I can't believe this."

I was trying to calm my mom down as I felt panic set in within my own body. I then asked her the dreaded question, "Did the ambulance team say anything about his condition?"

Through the ebbs of her panting, I heard, "They said they'd do the best they could."

Not more than an hour later, as I was attempting to get back home, my cell phone rang again. "Deb, where are you?" I heard the somber voice of my husband.

"I'm on the train heading back north. I'm almost there. It's Dad, isn't it? Harry, you promised you'd never hold anything like this from me, right?"

Through my husband's sadness I heard, "He's gone, Deb. I'm so sorry. I'll pick you up at the train station so you don't have to drive."

Without hesitation and almost screaming I replied, "No, no you won't. My car's at the station, so I'll drive. I need to drive."

"Okay. We're all at the hospital. Please come here instead. I love you and drive safe."

My dad was a deacon in the Catholic Church, and I knew he studied hard for this. What I didn't know was his struggle to become a deacon as an African American. I heard about this during his eulogy given by a long-time family friend, Father Tom. He talked about my dad not immediately being accepted by others in the church for this position. He discussed my dad's faith and how he wasn't going to let other humans decide God's will for him. My dad had struggles due to his race but never made that an issue for his children. I wish I could sit down with my dad now and swap stories and lessons on racism and prejudice. My dad protected us from this in some way, and I don't exactly know why. I can only guess that he felt we had something stronger. We had our faith and trust in the Almighty Lord. And with His armor, nothing prevails against you.

I love my dad with all my heart. I see him every time I notice that the hue in the sky is a tint of orange and lies against the dawn. This was the color of the sky the morning after he was embraced in God's arms. It was absolutely beautiful.

On May 1, 2017, I woke to an ordinary day and a short "to do" list in mind. The day was gray with a hint of warmth. I buzzed around the living room and kitchen area as I heard the footsteps of my husband and son coming down the stairs. I said my good mornings with a cheery smile and reached up to give both of them a morning kiss. I turned quickly to look in the refrigerator to figure out what we would have for breakfast. With my head in the frig, I immediately realized I could better make this decision with a good hot cup of coffee. I headed to the coffee machine to make the first cup of the day – the best cup. Still lingering in the kitchen with coffee now in hand, I picked up my iPhone and began to read through email messages, including social media pages.

And there it was, a public post asking if anyone had seen my 48-year-old cousin Christine in the last 24 hours. I glanced at the picture of her on the post, and then a separate picture of her car with the license plate number. *What?* I thought. *This can't be true. It's got to be some sort of cruel spam.* I ran to the living room to show my husband. "Do you think this is for real?" I asked impatiently.

My husband read the post twice then handed me back my phone. "I don't know," he replied. "Why don't you call Christine's cell phone to see if she answers."

I dialed Christine's cell phone several times. *Answer, please answer.* The phone barely rang then went straight to voicemail. I left a message to please call me. I quickly dialed my Aunt Mary's home phone. Christine is her daughter-in-law. She married my cousin Brent 16 years ago. They were a mixed-race couple and had a loving relationship. They didn't have any children and filled their life with family, friends, work, golf, their dog, shopping and visits to the beach. My Aunt Mary answered the phone hastily and told me she wasn't sure what exactly was going on. "I'll call you, Deb, when I hear anything," she said. I hung up the phone with an uneasy feeling. Aunt Mary seemed upset and tense.

It was too hard to just sit and wait for a phone call. My husband and I jumped in the car and went out to look for Christine. We headed to the local train station, as our thought was that maybe she just needed to get away for a while. We had the picture of her car with the license plate number, and used it to search through the line of cars at the train station. As we descended the hill at the station, I spotted a car. "There it is!" I shouted to my husband. He slowed the car and pulled up so we could read the license plate number. My head sunk as we compared the numbers aloud. No match.

We continued our search through the hundreds of cars at the station. As we were looking through the cars, my cell phone rang. "Hello, where are you?" my sister Tina asked.

"Harry and I are at the train station looking for Christine. Did you see the post this morning?" I responded.

"Yes, yes I did. Why don't you come to Mom's house right now? I'm here with her."

Harry and I pulled into my mom's driveway and noticed Tina holding the front screen door open for us to come in. We walked into the living room and before we could say a word, Tina said, "We lost her. Christine died."

My knees buckled as I began to shout, "No, no, no!" With tears streaming down my face, I ran into the sitting room to see my mom sitting in her chair with her face in her hands. My sister and husband came into the room behind me. "What happened?" I desperately asked my sister.

"Christine took her life," she stated. "We don't know all the details, but I was at Aunt Mary's when she found out. It's confirmed."

My family comes together in both great times and in tragedy. My sister Sue and her children arrived at

Mom's soon after, and later that evening my Aunt Mary, Brent and a few of his friends arrived too. Brent walked into the kitchen worn, broken and despondent. The family unintentionally formed a hug line with very few words spoken. We individually embraced Brent and shared his grief.

Nobody understands how someone who has a loving marriage, home, great career, family and friends could feel there was no other option for them besides suicide. That's the challenge with mental illness. Sometimes there's a mask that is worn to protect the person and the person's loved ones. Christine opened our eyes to this challenge. She made us realize that although it may appear all is well on the outside, the inside is what matters. I keep Christine close to my heart and in my prayers.

In March 2018, it was a perfect family morning. The television as usual was on in the kitchen, and my son HJ, husband Harry and I were all gathered around the island. Courtney was at school rounding out her senior year at college. Harry was feeling the best he had in twenty years. Two weeks prior, my niece Gina and he went through a successful kidney transplant. For whatever reason, there seemed to be a sense of urgency this particular morning. My husband was intent on getting things done that were on his list, simple things like renew the Sirius subscription, follow up on emails, and go through the pile of mail. HJ was feeling hurried as he was going to the gym to work out. He kissed his dad goodbye, told him he loved him and was off. I ventured into the home office to follow up on emails from the nonprofit board I was chairing. Harry moved from the kitchen island to the living room couch to finish reading emails.

Within 15 minutes, I heard a curt moaning sound. I ventured to the living room but Harry wasn't there on the couch. I looked over towards the kitchen and saw him grabbing the island. I ran over, embraced him, and said, "Breathe, honey, breathe." I thought I saw an acknowledgement that he understood me. I ran to get the phone and dialed 911. It was another out-of-body experience. The man who answered the phone asked a bunch of questions and then told me how to do CPR. He said an ambulance was on the way.

Later sitting in the first pew at my husband's funeral, it hit me—the person I fell in love with in 1973, dated for 15 ½ years, and then married for nearly 29 years, was no longer part of this earth. I will never hear him say "I love you" again or tease me. No more silly arguments over mundane topics. No more looking across the room at family gatherings with a special glance. No more shoulder to cry on or to share intimate feelings and challenges. And no opportunity to say I'm sorry—for all the things I did that I shouldn't have, and all the things I didn't do and should have. And the deepest pain, witnessing our children's realization that Dad was gone.

When we were in college, I wrote Harry a poem called "Montana Moon." He was studying in Montana and I was studying in upstate New York. We were hardly able to see each other. I found that poem while cleaning up a year after he passed and re-read it. It has so much more meaning now that Harry has left this earth. I believe the poem was written for this time now versus when we were in college. We just didn't know what was in front of us. But God knew. He always does.

Montana Moon

Is the moon the same there
As it is here?
I believe so.
Every time I look above, I can see you.
I do not have to wonder what you are doing,
for I know.
I do not have to wonder what you are feeling,
for I know that too.
Even though we are separated,
we are <u>one</u> in the moon.
For you see, there is but one moon in the universe,
when you are looking at the moon, and I am looking at the moon,
we are looking at each other.
I can truly see you.
If it is law, or faith, or fate that we be apart,
so let it be!

But "they" cannot take away our moon.
The moon possesses the same qualities as does our relationship;
the secretness, uniqueness, distance, invigorating, warmth, mystery, and the beauty.
My only wish is that the moon were <u>not</u> so distant, as you are, that the moon were not so mysterious, as you are, and that the moon stay forever and ever, as I hope you do.
I LOVE YOU BABE, and I can see this love in the moon.

D. Russell
1/11/1982
1:30 am

About a year after Harry passed, Mom was diagnosed with rectal cancer. We had just celebrated Christmas in our home in Orlando. Mom desperately wanted to get to Florida, so we surprised her with a trip for Christmas. My sister Tina, my niece Jessica, and another niece from Atlanta, Amanda, and her family joined us, as did our family from Miami, my cousin Paul, and his partner Doug. We had a grand time. My children and our pup Frenchy were with us, so it felt like we were exactly where we were meant to be. My children will tell you that my type-A personality kicked in and I was anxious and hyper—but I like to relish in the positive of the gathering. We celebrated with our traditional feast of fish dinner prior to Christmas Day, had great conversations, and laughed the night away.

I noticed Mom was not as lively as usual and seemed a bit withdrawn. She asked us for cream to help with what she perceived as an issue with hemorrhoids. When we returned home, she became weaker and we rushed her to the emergency room. She was admitted and they gave her a blood transfusion and scheduled a colonoscopy. The hemorrhoids were a mass. A biopsy confirmed it was malignant.

Mom started her chemotherapy and radiation therapy with determination. The doctors were confident she could pull through this with the love and support of her family. There was hope. I visited Mom one day at her home as she was going through treatment. I entered her sitting room and she was sitting in her recliner chair, her black and grey knit shawl spread across her lap and wearing her lime green sweatsuit to keep warm. The wooden electric fireplace was on. The small table next to the chair had a cup of tea that was now cold. The television mounted on the wall was playing in the background. She seemed down and not as talkative as she usually was during our visits. I heard myself talking to fill the air. I suddenly stopped and looked at my dear, sweet mother. "Mom, you remember when Harry was trying to get clearance for his kidney transplant and they found the mass in his chest?" I ask.

"Yeah, I remember," she replied without making eye contact.

I continued, "Well, I got down on my knees and begged God to make the mass be an infection or something we could easily clear up, so it wouldn't interfere with the transplant. And it seemed like forever for the doctor to call with the results. I finally lost patience and just called him." I felt my Mom now staring at my face. I looked into her eyes and said, "The doctor apologized for not calling sooner. He said it was nothing, nothing at all to worry about."

My Mom smiled as she whispered, "Isn't that wonderful, dear? The power of prayer."

I fought back tears and lovingly stared at my mom. "Yes, Mom, but it's more than that. I should've had enough faith to pray to make it *nothing*. I never prayed to make it *nothing*. But God made it nothing." My mother looked at me and shook her head affirmatively.

Mom passed to God about a month after that conversation, on her 82nd birthday. I feel her presence constantly. She was my very best friend. I know I was loved unconditionally, and she taught me that faith, family and friends is everything.

"Worthy are you, our Lord and God, to receive glory and honor and power, for you created all things, and by your will they existed and were created." (Revelation 4:11, ESV)

I can look back over the last few years and ask why I lost so many people I love in such a truly short time. Each life is precious, and each life has purpose. We are known to God before birth, and our death in this earthly world is inevitable. God comforts the grieving and provides healing for our hearts. He carries us. Some things happen in this world and directly impact us in ways we will never understand. Not now. Perhaps not ever. However, we pray for eternal life where pain, suffering and loss are no longer. We pray for a time when justice and generosity are part of our being. We pray for the Lord, our Savior, to rescue us.

> *"For you formed my inward parts; you knitted me together in my mother's womb. I praise you, for I am fearfully and wonderfully made. Your eyes saw my unformed substance; in your book were written, every one of them, the days that were formed for me, when as yet there was none of them." (Psalm 139:13-14, 16, ESV)*

CHAPTER **8**

God's Bigger Plan

There was the smell of fresh, crisp air that day in Boston. The sun was shining and the sky was blue. I had flown in from New York that morning with the hopes of presenting a new organizational structure for my division. This was yet again another merger that had taken place between my company and a large financial institution, although this one was a "merger of equals" versus a takeover. I was the managing director of a financial reporting group, and the proposal I put forth to the newly combined senior executive team was to merge the two financial analytics reporting groups from both firms, and have a vertical structure reporting to me. I was told it was a sound idea and that I would be given an opportunity to present this structure to the new powers at the helm.

I usually dressed somewhat conservative in my line of work – business suits, stockings, low heel pumps. This day was no exception. I remember entering the conference room, not that large but decorated with expensive leather chairs, a lovely wood table, placemats and all the other trimmings of a fancy boardroom. There were probably about ten executives sitting around the table. There was a seat for me next to my current business manager, who had previously told me he was going to be "neutral" in this meeting. I took my seat and attempted to say hello to anyone with whom I could make eye contact. I had met them all previously, but given the vibe in this room I was clearly a stranger. I had worked tirelessly on this presentation and the executive team seemed to be supportive, by assigning me someone from the other company who could help with ideas, structure and format. This gesture gave me hope that the new structure would seed some discussion and perhaps a better business outcome.

I went through the presentation without interruption. From time to time, as I looked up from my presentation book, I noticed most heads were staring down at their copies. I had an hour to make the presentation. There were diagrams and charts along with comments to explain how the organization could be structured. At the end of the presentation, a question came from one of the women executives. "Does this mean you would actually report to our boss if we did this?"

A firm voice came over me as the words came out one at a time, "Yes it does." The niceties were exchanged, and I was politely dismissed from the room.

I distinctly remember walking down a long corridor, searching for the elevator button that could not come soon enough. I descended to the lobby and walked across the shiny marble floor to the exit doors. I couldn't wait to leave that stately building in Boston. As soon as I got outside, I looked up at the bright sky with the sun shining and took a deep, long breath. It was not a sigh of relief but of sadness. Standing there on the paved sidewalk, I realized that I had just wasted months of my life putting together a proposal that was never going to be taken seriously. The decision had already been made before I stepped into that boardroom. The only problem was – they forgot to tell me! What I didn't know at that time was that I had my plan, but God had a bigger plan.

Jeremiah 29:11 (ESV) says, *"For I know the plans I have for you, declares the Lord, plans for welfare and not for evil, to give you a future and a hope."* This is one of the most popular verses amongst Christians. We often quote it to each other when we are unsure of God's plan for our future. It's often used at graduation ceremonies, to encourage graduates that the future is bright as long as God is walking alongside of them.

God used the prophet Jeremiah to reveal His plans to the Israelites after their exile from Jerusalem to Babylon. But do you know how many years it took before the Israelites returned to Jerusalem from the first exile to Babylon? Seventy years. Think about that. This meant possibly a few generations having passed from the time of the exile. Since prophesy was the only way God spoke to His people besides an audible voice or calling, prophesy was all they had to rely upon to verify what He was saying was true. God used prophets throughout both the Old and New Testament. Although this gift is not always used within the church today, it can be an incredible way God can use ordinary people to communicate His message—even if the message will take some time to come to fulfillment. The prophet Jeremiah also got his share of attacks. Jeremiah was always competing against other prophets who wanted to speak untruths for the sake of their own personal gain.

I can only imagine how difficult it was to be a prophet back in those days. All that chatter in the midst of what God was actually saying. It must have been downright confusing for people to distinguish between what God was saying and what people made up in their own immature attempts to get attention. The messages were often God's heart for his people, but some of those messages were far from positive. Prophets were often tasked with communicating God's wrath or judgment in a world who had forgotten God, and had instead built false idols they worshipped. This is why prophets were often despised, ridiculed and often killed.

But can you imagine what all those people thought when generation after generation of people came and went and the revelation never came? After many years had passed, those same young people, now older people, were left scratching their heads, asking themselves, "Did we get this wrong?" But like Jesus' birth, it came when people least expected it, and in the way they least expected. And it came when God said it would come.

God has known us since the beginning of time. Earlier in Jeremiah 1:5 (New International Version [NIV]), it says, *"Before I formed you in the womb I knew you, before you were born I set you apart...*" We all have been set apart for God's plan and purpose. Although I tried to control the plan to reorganize in a way I thought would lead to an ideal situation, God had His way that day. I ventured into that boardroom thinking I knew what was best for my life and the company. God had another plan—*the* plan. It wasn't until many years later I would come to know and understand His plan.

After that meeting, the organizational structure for my division was solidified, and it was clear I would report to one of the executives in that meeting room that day in Boston. Afterwards, I met with my new boss and told her I just needed some time to think. I took a one-week vacation and decided that if this is what was meant to be, I would return to work with full heart, mind and spirit, reporting to my new boss. And I did just that, while also keeping an eye open for other opportunities, and talking to folks across the organization at all different levels. I returned to my new boss and a senior level position that involved strategy and new product development.

Prior to this merger, one saving grace was that the senior executives at my company believed I could do more for the firm, and assigned me a senior sponsor in the company to help me navigate and develop through my career. This sponsor happened to be a female senior executive vice president at the time we met. I remember our first private lunch meeting. We had dining services available in our building on Wall Street for clients and senior executive meetings. I greeted the servers who had worked there many years and was escorted to one of the private dining rooms on the floor. I quickly took a seat at the side of the table and waited for my sponsor to arrive to take the seat at the head of the table, which controlled the buzzer to notify the servers when a course was over or the meal had ended.

As I was sipping on my water to take the frog out of my throat, in walked a tall, thin, impeccably dressed white woman with a cheery smile, short brown pixie haircut, light makeup, and a string of beautiful pearls with matching earrings. "Hello there," she said in a pleasant voice. "I was asked by my boss to meet with you." (Her boss was the president of the company.) She continued, "My hope is that we get to really know one another. Who knows – we might end up good friends one day!"

I thought I was dreaming. Was I really meeting with one of the most senior women in our firm, and she's talking about perhaps one day becoming friends? *Oh, my goodness,* I thought. This woman was well respected in the organization as a strong leader, smart and fair, a people person. I considered myself very fortunate to be one of the individuals she carved out time to get to know. We proceeded to have a wonderful lunch discussing our family life, work life and everything in between. She asked me to really think about my top two or three goals, so we could have some focal points for our future conversations. Over the course of time, I found out what a true sponsor was all about. Someone once told me a mentor is someone you tell the good, bad and ugly to, and there is a back and forth in helping each other. A sponsor, however, is someone who can actually make things happen for you within the organization, as they usually have clout and respect. You can ask for or seek a mentor, but a sponsor generally finds you—there is no asking or seeking.

After the merger, my sponsor was aware of my career goals and disappointments surrounding the organizational structure, and told me it was time to prove I could do more for the company outside of the financial analytics gig I'd been associated with since I graduated college. She encouraged me to look for opportunities inside my broader business area, explaining that most of the skills I'd gained over my tenure are transportable and need to be leveraged across the firm. She was aware of a Chief Administrative Officer (CAO) role that would be available in another sector of the company, and encouraged me to apply for it. I did just that and got the job. I moved offices about three blocks away and started the new job in 2008, just before one of the most horrific financial crises in our history.

CAO responsibilities vary depending on the business you support. Initially, I had a team of about thirty individuals that helped to support training & development, legal, product development & strategy, real estate, etc. Many of the non-business direct functions reported to this position. The division was one of the larger businesses for this part of our organization, and the products offered were quite diverse. In hindsight, moving over to this sector was the best decision for my career trajectory. I grew in many aspects of my development and was given the opportunity to understand, at a granular level, the aspects of truly running a global business, and all of this happening at a time when the investment markets were unstable. We had an extraordinarily strong team of leaders and individuals around the world who knew their business and really helped one another. This culture of teamwork was amazing, and this group was able to get through the most difficult situations.

After two years, I moved out of the CAO role and eventually became business head for one of the business groups within this same division, and was later promoted to a larger client segment. The business roles included dealing directly with clients, which is something I always enjoyed. This was the last position I would hold in this sector of the company, about five years altogether, before I received the most unexpected phone call of my career. One day while sitting in my office reading emails, my assistant, Janet, popped her head in my office and alerted me that a senior executive from my prior sector was on the phone. The call was brief. The male executive asked how I had been doing, and requested a meeting to discuss a possible organizational change that was being contemplated.

I headed over to meet the senior executive who called me, and walked into a building that was quite familiar to me on Wall Street. The executive's assistant sat me in a small conference room outside his office. My nose started to run from nerves. I grabbed a tissue from inside my portfolio and was wiping when he entered the room. "Are you sick?" he asked with concern.

"No, allergies I think," I replied quickly.

He sat down and looked me in the eye. "First, I just want to apologize that we didn't listen to you when you presented the vertical organization structure for these products five years ago. We want to create a new division, and wanted to see if you'll consider being the head of this new team. It would include all aspects of the business, and it's a global role. It's basically implementing the plan you presented years ago, except it's much bigger now."

I couldn't believe my ears. What I said next was not of my own doing—it was absolutely the Holy Spirit at work. "There's no apology needed at all," I stated matter-of-factly. I heard my own voice saying, "You see, it was meant for me to go to a new sector to learn more, grow, and meet new people. I'm now a much better leader to do this assignment for you and the company. It was all meant to be."

I feel in my heart that this was truly a lesson for all of us. I've often thought about this entire situation. If I had it my original way, they would've accepted my proposal and created the group the way I had suggested. I wouldn't have had the perspective of knowing all the pieces to run a truly global business. One of the biggest factors was that my current job allowed me to travel both within and outside the US in a way that differed from my earlier travels, and my boss at the time told me that there are sub-cultures at each location and that you can't treat all of them the same. You have to spend time understanding the sub-cultures and how each fit in to the overall company culture. That was great advice, and upon having the chance to run my own broader business, the sub-culture understanding was key.

By waiting, I was able to hone my skills, sharpen my craft, and be even more valuable, not only to the other divisions with which I worked but also as a person. By waiting I developed patience, a trait of great value in any setting, professional or otherwise. I learned submission, because I had to accept the executive's decision whether I agreed with it or not. I learned that sometimes failing is winning delayed. In my mind, it looked as if I had failed by not obtaining a promotion in my profession. But God wanted to work in my heart first. He wanted me to be more like Jesus so I could be used in a more powerful way through my other jobs, but also to work in the executive's life when he apologized.

If he had apologized years earlier, it wouldn't have meant the same to me. I would have allowed bitterness and resentment to take root in my heart, and that apology would've been a bunch of meaningless words that didn't remove the ache that my presumed failure would have occupied. But it didn't turn out that way at all. That apology made me realize there was a much bigger plan that couldn't be revealed to me at that time. We sometimes don't know what God is doing in our lives. Job loss, illness, a crumbling marriage, the loss of loved one. Anything can happen when we least expect it, and it makes us question God's purpose for it or His timing. But thankfully we serve a "God who orders our steps," knew us before we were born, and knows us so intimately that He knows what we're going to do before we do it. Although I didn't know it at the time, I can take solace in the fact that God had me in the palm of His hand that day, just like He has me in the palm of His hand all the days of my life.

And I remain a thankful, humble servant.

CHAPTER 9

India

In late September 2015, I was given the opportunity to visit our company offices in India. The Operations team there supported some of the products we deliver to clients. Our head Technology manager Lydia and I would travel together. I've known Lydia for many years. She's a wonderful woman. Lydia is about my age, another woman of color (Chinese), intelligent and trustworthy. She stands barely five feet tall, has short salt and pepper hair, and is a walking brain when it comes to technology. After twenty hours in the air, we stopped in Singapore to visit our local offices before continuing our trip. During our stopover in Singapore, Lydia arranged a dim sum lunch with her soon to be daughter-in-law and her future in-laws. "I want you to join my future family for lunch," she casually asked me on the way to our hotel.

"Really, I don't want to intrude," I replied. "Spend some time with your family. I need to catch up on emails."

"Nonsense. You're not going to sit in a hotel in Singapore by yourself. Come to lunch and have some good food with us."

We entered a restaurant inside a high-rise building with other stores and offices. The building had the feeling of an indoor shopping mall. In one corner of the layout, the restaurant was buzzing with excitement. As we entered, I noticed the massive size of the room, round tables, and beautiful colors. Lydia's family was already seated when we walked in. There were about ten people, including Lydia's future daughter-in-law, who jumped up to greet us. We exchanged greetings and sat to begin this wonderful dining experience.

I truly didn't know what to expect. Lydia helped me along the way. There's a group dynamic in selecting the dishes to share. The meal is served on small plates in the center of the table. The inner table spins around so the food can be delivered to each person sitting at the large outer table. The mature woman to my right was smiling and gesturing to me, asking if I wanted the next dish. Most of the table conversation was in Mandarin and Cantonese. I used my chopsticks to eat the delicious meal. I thought about one of my senior executives very early in my career, who once invited me to join her for lunch at a Chinese restaurant in New York City. She saw me struggling to copy her by using my chopsticks, and she just stopped in the middle of the lunch and gave me a quick tutorial. That lesson sure did come in handy over many, many years.

Lydia's daughter-in-law was excited about the upcoming wedding, and I enjoyed hearing stories about the details of this wedding that would take place in the US. It was also a welcome relief to have an English conversation with her, as most of the afternoon I was lost in translation. At the end of the lunch, one of the guests asked me if I spoke Mandarin. I shook my head no. She looked surprised. I was smiling, nodding and gesturing so much, she thought I understood. We both had a good giggle on that one.

We exited the restaurant and began our hugs and goodbyes. I then turned to Lydia and asked, "Do you think I can take a family photo of all of you?"

Lydia replied, "Wow, that's a great idea, I should've thought of that!" Everyone was excited to line up and smile for me as I took the picture.

As Lydia and I were heading back to our hotel, I thanked her from my heart. It was more than a lunch. It was a cultural experience. I so enjoyed the excitement, imagery, food, language and love that I witnessed within this family. It made me long to be with my family around a large table, talking, eating and just enjoying each other. I felt honored to be there.

We landed in Chennai, India a couple of days later, and I was not prepared for another cultural experience. Located in South India, Chennai is one of the largest cultural, economic and educational centers in the region[1]. Our visit included stops in both Chennai and Pune. Pune is on the western side of India; it's the second

---

[1] All factual information in this section retrieved from Wikipedia on January 15, 2021.

largest city in the state of Maharashtra after Mumbai, and is the eighth most populous city in India. Pune is known for its education, technology, and automobile and manufacturing hubs. Our days were filled with one-on-one and group meetings, town halls, visits to the site offices, strategy sessions with the senior executives in the regions, and box lunches along the way to keep everyone on schedule – especially us. India is a hospitable culture, and guests are made to feel incredibly special.

One colleague who was staying at our hotel on a longer-term assignment asked Lydia and me if we wanted to visit the market and tour the city. Of course we did! The one aspect we weren't prepared for was the mode of transportation. We stepped outside and hailed down two small open-air box-style vehicles. The motors were loud, and the smell of fumes greeted us as the drivers pulled up. Our colleague negotiated the price, turned to hand us a scarf to cover our faces from the fumes, and off we went. Wow, what an experience. There were people everywhere, riding on scooters, walking, running. There was a family of four hanging on a moving scooter that appeared to be built for two. Amazing. The market was crowded and busy, with vendors lined up on the streets. I won't forget the pungent smell in the air in one particular area as we zipped by. And the faces, these beautiful people who stare and then smile. They knew we were visitors, and we were honored guests in their country. They were humble, and some extremely poor, but their spirits ignited like fire.

The evening after our tour through town, two of our staff members, Jeba and Agila, took us shopping and then joined us for dinner at our hotel for a traditional Indian meal. I was so happy to have them with us to teach us about the clothing, food and etiquette. Before leaving for my trip, one great piece of advice I received from a woman colleague who had visited the region prior was to leave the heels at home. I was also told to pack light and comfortable clothes. Great advice all the way around. The office attire of the women local staff was sensational. Most women wore traditional colorful saris with sandals or flat shoes, and the men wore dark slacks with collared dress shirts. I was keen to buy a traditional Indian outfit during our shopping trip to take home as a great memory.

The shopping trip was full of fun and laughter. Lydia and I both tried on colorful garments and noticed the sizes ran smaller than what we were accustomed to in the States. At one point I couldn't fit my head into the opening of one top, and it became quite the chuckle. "My head is too big," I shared with my colleagues as I exited the dressing room. Lydia admitted to having the same problem. We had a good laugh. I did finally find a beautiful black, gold and red outfit that had the matching top and pants. I bought one for my daughter too. Mission accomplished.

It was now time for the four of us to venture back to the hotel for dinner. Jeba and Agila took command, ordering the food they felt we would best enjoy. We were more than grateful to be in their expert hands. We capped our meal with delicious hot tea. As our server placed the meal in front of us, Jeba leaned over and whispered, "Would you like to eat your Indian food in the traditional manner?" Lydia and I both nodded our heads affirmatively. "We will use our hands to eat," Jeba stated with a smile. So here we went, eating with our hands, drinking hot tea, hearing lovely stories about Agila's son and Jeba's family. The evening flowed like a beautiful symphony.

All of a sudden, I felt a type of euphoria wash over me. I had exhaled in a way I hadn't done in years. It felt peaceful. *What was it?* The dimly lit restaurant with candles at our table? The delicious food that was pleasing to the palate? The company of Lydia, Jeba and Agila? It was all of it. It was India. After experiencing the day with the people, the places and all the cultural awakenings, this dinner gave me an opportunity to take it all in and appreciate it. Another gift from God, to realize how different life is outside my corner of the world. To feel as though sometimes I have so much but perhaps not enough of the things that really matter. It was a feeling I will never forget. I told my children about it when I returned. It was magical. I know I left India a different person. A better person. A more grateful person.

> *"Above all, keep loving one another earnestly, since love covers a multitude of sins. Show hospitality to one another without grumbling. As each has received a gift, use it to serve one another, as good stewards of God's varied grace." (1 Peter 4:8-10, ESV)*

CHAPTER 10

Woodloch Women

Grand Central Station in New York City is a beautiful building, and I spent many hours in it while commuting from upstate New York. It's also a great hub to meet business acquaintances and friends for breakfast, lunch or dinner. In spring 2005, I had a breakfast meeting with Alan. We decided to make it convenient for both of us, so we met at Naples in Grand Central. Alan is a great friend and we've worked together at the same company in prior years, he on the sales side and I on the service side. Alan and I travelled with the extended team on business and worked hard to win new business for our company. Every time I called him, he would begin our conversations with a long, drawn-out, "Baaaaaaker, what's up?"

Alan eventually moved into a different industry, commercial real estate; however, after his initial move we kept in touch. With Alan being Jewish and married with twins, I always found our conversations to be uplifting and with a lot of knowledge shared. At breakfast this particular day, we had a lot of catching up to do. Alan was now settled in the new job, so I wanted to know how that was progressing. I had no doubt he was a huge success, as he always worked with determination and a standard of care. We also had to swap pictures of the children and all that good stuff. He always had fun things on the agenda, so I asked what his plans were for the upcoming spring break. His face lit up. "Have you heard of a place called Woodloch Pines in Pennsylvania?" he asked with enthusiasm.

The rest of the breakfast was spent talking about this place. Alan's family had been traveling there for many years. Woodloch is a family resort with housing, food and fun. Folks actually get dressed for dinner, and there's an activity schedule to keep everyone in the family happy. "Sounds great, I need to check this place out," I responded enthusiastically. And I did. Several years in a row, in fact, renting houses with extended family members and friends.

The year 2009 rolled around and a milestone birthday was staring at me. *How in the world could I be turning 50!?* Oh well, it happens. I felt in my heart I wanted to do something quite different and special. By this time, Woodloch had extended the resort and built a health and wellness spa. *Okay, I've got it,* I thought. *I'll plan a women's retreat at Woodloch.* Over the years, I've felt the benefits of women helping women and just hanging out. There's a special bond of love and respect when you have shared experiences and goals.

This weekend birthday celebration turned out to be an experience that will forever impact my life. I was joined by nine fabulous women: my mom, sisters Tina and Sue, one of my best friends Natalie, Aunt Mary, cousin Christine, my niece Gina, Aunt Shirley, and my 88-year-old grandmother, Nana Grace. I wanted this to be an experience for them more than me. It gave me delight to see them having a good time, laughing and just being together.

The celebration was guided by an itinerary, of course, given my type-A personality. We started the weekend with room assignments and birthday t-shirts left on the beds in each room. Each guest pre-selected a spa treatment and an activity; painting, crafting, yoga, etc. We had great meals and beverages along the way. The "on your own" time included room for hiking, swimming and fishing. I also planned a private cooking demonstration and subsequent meal. One evening we were picked up by a van to venture to an on-premise show – this gave us an opportunity to all wear our matching birthday t-shirts.

Part of the itinerary included a gathering in my room one evening for wine and cheese. There's a small sitting area where my guests squeezed in and relaxed. Before I realized it, I no longer had control of the itinerary. They planned this part of the event. Beforehand, each guest was asked not to give me a physical gift, but instead consider a donation to a favorite charity. They did that and beyond. As we settled into my sitting room, the snacks and beverages were plenty, arranged on a small table in a self-serve style. There was a couch and dining chairs forming a circle.

After the chatter of excitement of sharing the day began to die down, Aunt Mary explained that each guest had something to share with me. Suddenly, the room became very quiet and serious. There was some comic relief as my sister, Sue, began to read her script that she framed for me to keep. Throughout the script she compared our different personality styles in hosting, jumping on trains to get to work, Christmas decorations and gratuities. The group was roaring with laughter as her delivery was nothing short of a professional stand-up comic. My sister Tina used the letters in my first, middle and last name to create a rhyming poem describing our relationship. It was beautiful. Aunt Mary also wrote a lovely poem indicating my life song was a blessing from above, and my niece Gina thanked me for always making her feel first in my life.

By this time, the tissues were flowing and what started with laughter was now peppered with tears of joy and gratitude. Aunt Shirley then shared her poem which began at my birth, through college and marriage, and tied it in a bow exclaiming it was all from God. Amen to that. Through tears, Natalie talked about our loving friendship through the years, and added some humor when she admitted being jealous when I spend more time with another train friend. Christine talked about the value of paying it forward and how grateful she was to be included with this group of women. Nana Grace gave me a copy of the poem "Grandma's Pearls of Wisdom" by Becky Netherland. I keep a copy on my bedroom nightstand to this day. Mom wrote two poems; one was humorous, talking about how I loved wearing a red wig, disliked ballet, had Harry over for dinner too often, and it all ended up just fine. Her other poem was more serious, as she's the person who knew and understood me the best:

My goodness look who's fifty, it's so hard to believe,
she's always worked so very hard, for what she wanted
to achieve.
She married the man she always loved, and beautiful
children she had two,
and climbed the ladder of success, my how the years
just flew.
Family is her priority, and the love of God her guide,
she filled her life with giving and filled her family with pride.
She's traveled the world over, but always her heart was here,
to sit by the fire, a glass of wine, and all her loved ones near.
So this is a special birthday, she is celebrating this year,
and we're all thrilled to be included, because we love you
so much, my Dear.
                                        —*Irene Russell, 10/9/09*

Just as I was about to gain control of my emotions, another sheet of paper came out. My sister, Tina, explained that my daughter Courtney sent this along for my birthday. She was 13 at the time, so too young to attend this particular gathering. I opened the paper and read aloud. She joked about my nagging and my relentless nature at times, and then went on to say that

I'm special. She told the group her mom thinks they're special too. She asked the ladies to come back from this trip as close as sisters – and for the ones who are sisters, come back even closer. She then took my fifty years of life and broke it down in a numbers poem that included career, marriage, motherhood and more.

At the end of the evening, we gave each other longer, stronger hugs, as we all felt that our lives had fundamentally changed. Digging so deep and sharing in that way was the greatest gift anyone could ask for on any birthday. When my guests left my room that night, I went into my luggage bag and pulled out the video camera. I was trying to get some of the weekend on film to have as a keepsake. On this particular night, I wanted to record my feelings. I wanted to remember what it feels like to receive so much love and joy. I wanted to thank God for making me realize that the place, the food and beverages, and the entertainment are great, but the people are greater. When we returned home, we could hardly talk about it to others without having tears of joy in the storytelling. When I reminisce about that birthday celebration, I see the hand of God in my snapshot images. There was a reason God pulled us together in celebration that weekend. We would need each other more than we realized. I remember the ending of Aunt Mary's poem saying, "I for one can't wait and will be ready for when you will turn 60!"

Within those ten years, each one of us had life-changing events. By the time I celebrated my 60th birthday, we carried the grief of losing my grandmother Nana Grace, my mom, cousin Christine, Aunt Mary's husband, and my own husband. Sue and Natalie decided to separate from their husbands. Gina would donate her kidney in an attempt to save my husband's life. Aunt Shirley would leave her life in the City and relocate to upstate New York. And Tina was in the thick of dealing with grief across our family. We now have an even stronger bond knowing that we need our faith, our family and our friends to walk through the fires of life.

And let's not forget He who carries us.

"But Ruth said, 'Do not urge me to leave you or to return from following you. For where you go I will go, and where you lodge I will lodge. Your people shall be my people, and your God, my God.'" (Ruth 1:16, ESV)

I love the Book of Ruth. It's one of my favorite Bible stories. There are many aspects to this relatively short book. Ruth was a Moabite woman who married a Jewish man. Ruth's husband and his brother both died. Prior to this, Ruth's mother-in-law Naomi lost her husband, leaving her a widow. Naomi had asked both her daughters-in-law to return to their home country after the deaths of their husbands, while she planned to return to Judah. Ruth wouldn't hear of it. She insisted on staying with Naomi and giving up her culture, beliefs and family. It was a test of true loyalty and faith, and Ruth was blessed by God for it. After Ruth returned to Bethlehem with Naomi, the Lord allowed Ruth to remarry and give birth to a son named Obed, who became the grandfather of King David. This genealogy is tied to the birth of Jesus in the New Testament.

I feel the loyalty and sisterhood of the women in my life, not only those who attended that 50th birthday celebration but beyond. I hope they feel that from me too. It's a notion that they really care about your well-being, your happiness, your peace. That they'll go out of their way to help you. That they'll sacrifice on your behalf.

Above all, they're the ones who pray for you.

CHAPTER 11

Stranger Encounters

Marsha

I had arrived in Dublin exhausted by the trip from New York. Usually I have no problem sleeping on planes, but for whatever reason I wasn't able to get much sleep during this trip. I grabbed a taxi to my hotel room and was looking forward to settling down for a good night's rest. I entered the hotel to a very quaint setting that was a bit unexpected. I had been to Europe many times prior; however, my new assignment gave me an opportunity to visit clients and staff in Ireland for the first time. As I walked over to the reception counter to check in, I noticed a roaring fire against the wall that emitted a shimmery hue across the entire room. I was greeted with a lovely Irish accent as I was given my room assignment. The lobby area was set up with large, comfortable, stuffed leather chairs along with tables to sit your beverage or snack. The room was smaller than other lobbies I've visited, but bustling with activity as the guests settled into those cozy chairs for conversation. The elevators were towards the back of the room, so I made my way through the chairs to get to them.

I walked into my hotel room with all the standard amenities: queen bed, desk with chair, spacious bathroom, and windows overlooking a narrow street with a building across the way. The room was clean and tidy but not nearly as cozy as the lobby area. As I began to unpack my clothes for fear of a wrinkled week-long wardrobe, something dawned on me. My inner voice asked, *Why don't you go back downstairs and enjoy a glass of wine in front of that fireplace, then go to bed?* I had just turned 50 the month prior and it's true what they say—life changes after 50!

Needless to say, my clothes stayed in the bag, I grabbed my room key and handbag, and headed back downstairs. I was in luck – there were two empty cozy chairs around a small table in between them, close to the brimming fireplace. I only needed one side of that table, so I made my move to grab it. I settled in the chair and soon thereafter a woman with a tray in one hand approached me to ask if I would like a beverage. "Chardonnay, please," I said with a light sigh. Off she went to get it while I was beginning to feel the warmth of the fireplace and the relaxed atmosphere. Once my wine was delivered, I thanked the server and began to reach for my Blackberry to check on emails.

As I was reading, I felt someone standing over me. I thought the server had returned for some reason and I looked up to a smile. Startled, I let out a meek, "Hello?" A mature black woman with a round face, beautiful skin, wide brown eyes, a slender physique and a warm, bright smile had appeared. I made a quick assumption that she was American like me, until she began to speak in a similar accent to the receptionist. "May I join you, my friend?" I recalled her greeting.

All thoughts of stranger danger went out of my head as I responded without a second thought, "Yes, of course, please sit down." I caught myself stifling the automatic outstretched arm, hard handshake, and direct look in the eye that came with business protocol, realizing it wasn't appropriate for this warm setting.

The woman introduced herself as Marsha. She lived in the hotel next door at that time, and loved coming to this hotel for the lobby atmosphere. She was born in the Americas, but moved to the United Kingdom more than 45 years ago. Marsha asked me what a middle-aged Black American girl was doing in a hotel lobby all by herself on a weeknight. We laughed and I told her about my job and the opportunity to visit other countries, and admitted this was my first time in Dublin. She asked about my family and I shared that I was married with two teenage children, and told stories about each of them. We talked at length about the hardships of trying to balance everything: family, career, life in general. Then my husband's voice came into my head: *Don't forget to ask about them. That's the real reason they're asking about you; they have a story to share.* So I leaned forward in the cozy chair and looked at Marsha. "Are you married?" I asked. "Do you have any children? What about your career?"

She let out a slight smile and began her story. She started with her survival from breast cancer. It was a journey that changed her life. She talked about losing her hair and going through extensive treatments. Marsha made it clear that this didn't define her. The cancer was a part of her life, but it was not her entire life. She had one daughter who she loved, and she casually mentioned her daughter's father's name who happened to be a world-famous rock star! In her earlier years, Marsha acted and was a musician herself, pretty connected to celebrities we read and hear about in the music industry. Wow! I couldn't believe this chance encounter was happening to me. What are the odds of meeting someone like Marsha in another country, in a hotel lobby, after a seven-plus hour flight? Amazing!

At the end of our conversation, she asked if I would wait as she ran back to her hotel to get something. I did. She reentered the lobby with a book in hand. "I wrote this book in 2005. I've signed it for you. Please accept this as a gift," she stated as she handed it to me. I stood up from my chair and hugged her as I accepted the gift. I said goodbye to Marsha and headed towards the elevator to go back to my room to unpack and sleep. Upon entering my room, I flipped to the title page of the book and felt a tear fall down my cheek. Marsha had not only signed the book, but she had also inscribed, "Sometimes a chance meeting becomes a life change. Happy Reading. Love, Marsha 12 Nov 2009."

Ashok

In fall 2011, my assistant Janet and I hurriedly walked out of our office building on Barclay Street to grab a taxi. We had to get to a restaurant a few blocks away for an important meeting. We walked in to the sounds of a busy, downtown New York scene, where there was clamor of conversation, servers meandering through narrow walkways, and the bustling of people trying to get to their seats. The restaurant reminded me of the good old-fashioned 1980s vibe. Lots of brass and glass. There were highly sought-after tables next to the floor-to-ceiling windows that overlooked the activity on the sidewalks of downtown Manhattan. Wooden tables were aligned in a way that created tight walkways. The bar was against the opposite wall of the windows and it was huge. Some folks were sitting at it as though their day had already ended. Others were at tables clearly trying to conduct business, while yet others were there as tourists, family or friends gathering for a great meal and conversation. *A nice mix of people*, I thought.

Neither Janet or I had ever been to this restaurant; however, we needed to pick a venue for a special meeting, and it had great reviews. We were lucky to be seated at one of those tables next to the windows as it was a clear, sunny day. After about ten minutes of waiting and sipping on our iced teas, our guest walked through the door. I saw him speak to the hostess and then look across the dining room to find us. We had never met before, so in my email to him I gave him a little description of myself. Janet and I were not that hard to spot, as there weren't that many African American and Guyanese women in the restaurant that day. I started to wave my right hand in the air just as he turned and began to approach us with a bright, warm smile.

He seemed tall to me, although he was in essence not that much taller than I. He was a very handsome young man, with olive colored skin and dark brown hair, neatly dressed in a sports jacket, khaki pants, dockers and pressed dress shirt. He illuminated a pleasant aura about himself. I noticed he was using a cane to help navigate his movements. We greeted each other and sat down to lively conversation and a delicious lunch. His speaking tone was strong and friendly.

Our guest quickly segued into talking about a devastating event and how in minutes it fundamentally changed his life. He also talked about his family and how they needed to care for him physically, mentally and spiritually. He gave us details of the actual day it happened. Prior to his incident, he'd had a very good job in New York that afforded him the luxury to live independently in Manhattan. It took years of both physical and mental therapy for him to regain his zest for life. The incident had left him partially blind and needing assistance with walking. He was so excited on that lunch day, as he was in the final stage of publishing a book about his journey. He had a deep desire to share his story about his tragedy, as well as some of his critical childhood experiences. He wanted to help others who've suffered like him, and to provide hope that it can get better. Similar to my own upbringing and struggles as an African American growing up in a predominantly white neighborhood, he shared how it wasn't easy living in a predominantly white neighborhood as a young Indian boy. He was often taunted and teased for his brown skin and desire to be better by studying hard.

Before the lunch ended, I casually asked if he was dating or had a special person to share in his journey. He looked me squarely in the eyes, bent his lips forming that warm smile, and said, "Oh yeah, on top of everything else I told you, I'm gay."

I looked at Janet and her eyes were as wide as buttons. Janet then piped in while I was collecting my thoughts, and gently posed the question, "How has being gay been accepted by your family? I mean, being of Indian descent?" He made it clear that his parents loved him for who he was and that's what mattered to him.

We ended the lunch with hugs and promises to keep in touch and of course to buy the book once it was published. Before we parted, he joked that people often mispronounce his name. He then shared the correct pronunciation: "It's Ashok (A-Shoke). Rhymes with 'a Coke!'"

I did buy his book, nine years after that lunch, when I really needed it.

My company had offices all over the world, and it was quite fulfilling to be able to travel and meet people from all customs, cultures and ethnic backgrounds. In 2011 there was a local trip that had a tremendous impact on my life, a flight from Chicago to New York on an early Friday evening. The airport was packed and announcements about relinquishing your plane seat and checking bags versus carry-ons was abounding. Everyone seemed to be in a tremendous rush. There were food stations with long lines, and restaurants and bars in the airport that were packed to the gills.

I wheeled my carry-on over to an empty seat in the waiting area by my gate, and was relieved to get the chair after a long, hard day of meetings and presentations. The rule was if you left your seat, it was open game for anyone to swoop in, so I stayed put. Before I blinked the person next to me got up, and within two seconds an older Indian gentleman with a kind face, shorter stature, and slightly gray thin hair sat down next to me. He was a little frustrated. We smiled at each other and then began to make small talk about how busy the airport was on that day, and he shared the fact that he was on stand-by. "I really hope I get on this flight tonight; it's Friday and I want to get home," he stated. I nodded and agreed, and we shared what brought us to Chicago and how long we had been in town – true small talk.

The airline crew began to announce the boarding sequence, so I said goodbye and good luck as I wheeled my carry-on to the check-in counter. Slowly the line moved through the airport hangar until I saw a smiling face at the end saying "Welcome!" from the plane steward. I sat down in my seat, got settled and looked up the aisle at all the activity. From the corner of my eye, I noticed the older gentleman coming down the aisle. He got on the plane! Terrific! The gentleman made his way down the aisle and stopped at my seat. I smiled politely at him and said, "You made it, that's great!" He looked at me and smiled back. He then told me that he was in the seat right next to me! *How is that possible?* ran through my mind. "My name is Raj, by the way," he said as he shook my hand, made himself comfortable, and began his story.

He told me many things during that flight back to New York, but the one story that's impacted me the most was about his younger son who was now in his mid-thirties. It was the day of his eldest son's wedding, and he along with his wife and two sons had been gathered at a hotel in Washington DC for the wedding feast. His family was touring the Washington DC area while his younger son stayed at the hotel. The hotel contacted his elder son and stated there had been an emergency. His eldest son (the groom) had found his younger brother in his hotel room, lying prone and unresponsive on his bed, the victim of a devastating brain hemorrhage. This father explained the shock, pain and agony of this experience. His son surviving the devastating event, however, left him with some blindness, and needing assistance with walking. There were times of epileptic seizures and spotty memory recall. It also impacted his hearing.

Though there were many years of recovery and a tremendous life change for the entire family, there's a survival story here. His younger son was now living on his own in downtown Manhattan and thriving. His son understood that he was a changed person for the better. He still finds joy in his life despite the pain and suffering. Raj turned to me with determination and stated matter-of-factly, "You should meet my son, as he lives near your work. I think the two of you would get along fabulously." He took a small business card out of his carry-on bag and wrote a name and email address on it. "Here's my son's contact details," he said as he handed me the card.

When I returned to my office on Monday morning, I shared the story with my assistant Janet. I told her I felt compelled to meet Raj's son as I didn't think the encounter with Raj was coincidental. I asked Janet to join me, as she would really appreciate being included on this venture, and it also allowed me to have the "buddy system" as I would be meeting a stranger. Janet eagerly asked, "Who are we going to meet?" I rummaged through my briefcase to find the small business card with the scribbled writing from Raj. There in black letters was the name ASHOK with email address included.

Patty

In February 2017, my sister Sue and I attended a premiere in New York City for an upcoming television movie series. These premieres are wonderful experiences that I share with family and friends in order to let them know how special they are to me. We also just have an outright blast together. We plan a day or night out and enjoy each other's company, and have met some pretty fascinating people over the years. This particular event stands out in my mind as I always enjoy my sister's company. She has grit and humor, and she has this gift of understanding the true heart of people.

We walked into this fabulous ballroom where a cocktail hour was in progress. I was admiring the room with a view from the tall-towered windows, round tables with beautiful lilac linens, bright chandeliers, white and lilac rose centerpieces, and the lovely music playing in the background. I turned around and my sister was in a full conversation with a woman sitting in a chair, seemingly trying to get organized with red cell phone in hand. The woman's sweater matched the room with a darker shade of purple. Her hair was light brown, just below the shoulders, and her eyes were penetrating. Her makeup was fresh and she appeared to be enjoying the conversation with my sister.

I approached my sister as she stood up to introduce me to the woman. "Deb, this is Kathleen," Sue said with a bright smile on her face.

I extended my hand and said, "Hello, Kathy."

My sister's face was aghast. Before I could ascertain what happened, the woman sternly corrected me in a deep, raspy voice, "It's Kathleen!"

Sue gently took my elbow and moved me away as she told the woman it was a pleasure to meet her. As soon as we were out of earshot of the woman, Sue looked at me and let it rip. "You're not serious, are you? That's one of the most famous movie actors of our generation." She then shared the woman's last name, and it was clear I had made an embarrassing mistake. We couldn't help ourselves, and burst out in giggles. My sister likes to talk about my obliviousness any chance she gets.

The cocktail hour was wrapping up and now it was time to take our seats for lunch. We were given our table number on the way in, #3, right in front of the panel area. *Wow, what luck*, I thought. My sister and I took our seats, and I noticed there were about four other African American folks in a room of about 150. Unfortunately, this was the norm unless the premiere focused on African American actors or themes.

A woman with straight dark brown hair, soft eyes, about 5'5", wearing a knitted black belted skirt and top, arrived at our table. Her personality was warm and friendly. She possessed a certain energy that was noticed. Accompanying her was another woman with straight blonde hair and electric eyes, wearing a theme outfit in honor of the premiere, including a lace hat, gloves, and full makeup to look like the movie star. Later, we found out the two women were sisters, like us.

All of a sudden, it seemed as though we were getting visitors to our table. There was fluid conversation, and it was clear the other sisters knew many folks in the industry. Sue didn't hesitate to ask the table visitors for a picture, and they obliged. Another few minutes passed, and I noticed a bit of a fuss at the entrance door. The program staff was looking and pointing to our table. I leaned over and whispered to my sister, "I'm not sure we're supposed to be at this table. It seems to be a VIP table and they've run out of space in the front."

Without missing a beat, my sister leaned into me and said, "Pick up your fork and start eating your salad. Act like you belong and they won't come near us. We were assigned table #3." I did as I was told, and she was correct.

Through great conversation we found out that the name of the woman with the straight brown hair was Patty. She asked us what we did for a living and we reciprocated. It turned out she's a singer. Once she heard I was a board chair for a non-profit, she wanted to help. She gave me her email address and said to keep in touch. Sue and I left the event and headed for the elevators. We were like two children at Christmas, just plain giddy. It was a great afternoon. The food was fabulous, the atmosphere was lovely, but most importantly the people we met were so kind, especially Patty.

My sister turned to me in the elevator and said, "Now don't lose that email address Patty gave you. And take the time to follow up with her. She can help you." I smiled and agreed that I would follow up. All of a sudden my sister says, "You do know who you were sitting next to, right?"

I said, "Yes, she's a singer."

My sister rolled her eyes as she told me Patty's last name. "Yes, that's right, she's married to the famous tennis player. I can't believe you come to these events and don't know who's who." I smiled to myself as I believe that's the way God intended it to be. We are all equal. We don't move our seating because we feel lesser. We don't flaunt our power, wealth or connections because we have them. We look to raise each other up. Patty did that for us that day. She spent time with us and she wanted to know how she could help. Almost four years later, Patty and I are still connecting.

Are there really coincidences in the larger Kingdom of God? If God is in charge of everything, there are no coincidences. What we think are random events in life are actually placed there in God's foreknowledge. Think about what Genesis 1:1-5 (ESV) says:

"In the beginning God created the heavens and the earth. The earth was without form and void, and darkness was over the face of the deep. And the Spirit of God was hovering over the face of the waters. And God said, 'Let there be light,' and there was light. And God saw that the light was good. And God separated the light from the darkness. God called the light Day and the darkness he called Night. And there was evening, and there was morning, the first day."

If God is the One who set the Earth and life into being since the beginning of time, can't He handle who gets placed in our lives at different times?

God is omniscient, meaning He knows everything. If God knows everything before the beginning of time, there are no accidents. Ashok as well as his dad were in my life for a reason. Meeting Ashok and his father changed my life in a powerful way. If I hadn't met Ashok's dad on the plane, he never would've told me about his son. I would've never met his son and understood joy in a new way. The same can be said of my encounter with Marsha. She, like Ashok, had faced life-changing challenges she chose to overcome, to fill her life with family, friends and love. And in meeting Patty, where on the surface it seemed as though our lives run down quite different paths, we were connected in our love for our family and friends and trying to do our best to help others. I think back on that encounter with my neighbor George and my dad embracing at my backyard barbeque. That wasn't a chance meeting; that was designed by God. I have cheerful images of them now embracing in Heaven.

Joy isn't based on our circumstances, as Ashok and Marsha taught me. They showed me that no matter how desperate our circumstances may seem, we can choose to change them by seeing them through the lens of joy, or choose to see them with negativity through the things we've lost. In Ashok's case, he lost a vital life that his youth would've afforded him. But instead, he still had great joy and worked within the confines of his new situation.

Psalm 30:5 ESV says, "...*Weeping may tarry for the night, but joy comes with the morning.*" What will you choose today? Will you choose to see your circumstances with joy and positivity or negativity and despair?

The choice is ours.

CHAPTER 12

Israel

As an adult, I so look forward to Sundays; but as a child and young adult, Sundays were just not as fun and fulfilling. It was the end of the weekend, homework had to get finished, or prep for work had to start. I focused more on what I was leaving behind, like an exciting weekend, or what was in front of me like going back to school or work. My perspective on this day has matured with time, and now is much more in line with what God intended—a day of rest, a sabbath. Although I try to embrace every day with prayer and intentional focus, thoughts and acts that would be pleasing to the Lord, Sunday has become a day of deep reflection, repentance, worship, rest and prayer. I look forward to waking up and preparing my heart for church, even while getting dressed to leave the house. The car radio is off so I can reflect on what's ahead of me when I enter the church doors. I look forward to seeing the church family who I'm closer to now more than ever. The prayers, the songs, and most importantly the Word of the gospel radiates throughout my body. Afterwards, I may catch up with my relatives or other members of the church to eat a good meal and continue sharing, loving, being.

Once in 2017, after service one Sunday, my church tribe—my aunts, sister, niece and I—ventured off to one of our favorite brunch places. We so enjoyed this time to reflect on what was discussed at service, ask any clarifying questions in a safe, loving environment, and of course share good food and what was going on with our respective families. Sometimes we would allow ourselves to dream a bit and talk about those once-in-a-lifetime vacations and wish-list experiences. My aunts Mary and Shirley, sister Tina and niece Jessica talked at length about the possibility of a group trip to Israel. Our church sponsored a trip each year, and every time it was mentioned during church service we would look over at each other and smile. This would truly be a dream experience. When we first started to seriously discuss going, my husband was preparing for a kidney transplant, so a trip to Israel or anywhere else was out of the question at that time. This church trip to Israel has been occurring in March every year for the past several years. *When Harry gets better, I'll go to Israel with the tribe and the church*, I thought. That following March, Harry unexpectedly passed.

The Christmas after Harry passed, my children gave me a book about Israel. They felt the trip would be what I needed emotionally, spiritually and physically, after such a great loss for all of us. The next trip was scheduled for March 2019. I couldn't fathom going out of the country at this time. I also didn't want to leave my children alone without me to endure Harry's one-year anniversary in Heaven. The trip came and went as I continued trying to put the pieces of our lives back together. I didn't realize yet that the pieces were in front of me, not behind me.

We have our plans, and God always has the bigger plan. The only plan. He helps us make decisions as He knows what's in front of us. As it turned out, Mom passed away in March 2019 and I was there to hold her hand and tell her I loved her. More pieces to pick up, more pain to bear, yet more of a sense of being cared for, carried and loved. By fall of 2019, the buzz of the next trip to Israel was stirring in church again. This time the tribe was not as enthused as they'd been in the past. Much had happened during that time. I found myself praying about this trip. Something was drawing me to it – or better yet, Someone. I started to talk about the trip as a pilgrimage and not just an experience or vacation. To me, this trip would be like no other. I just felt it before I even signed up. The shocker was that I would be going alone on this trip. No husband, no children, no long-time friends, no tribe. Just the church family and me.

We left for our trip to Israel on March 5, 2020 and arrived at our first stop in Caesarea by the Sea after a layover in Istanbul, Turkey. It was beautiful in Caesarea. The trip itinerary was packed with many holy sites and

I was so looking forward to this pilgrimage. Dr. Bryan was our tour leader and his credentials—having lived in the Middle East and studied the lands, language, people and culture, and his love of the Bible—was a gift for all of us. I enjoyed the entire trip from top to bottom. There are areas we explored that changed the way I now think about this earthly life. It also awakened my senses to the more important eternal life. Seeing the Jordan River, floating in the Dead Sea, motoring across the Sea of Galilee, and leaving prayers at the Western Wall was incredible. Walking where Jesus walked, the Via Dolorosa, and touching the rock that shook when He died, are life-changing moments. I was not mentally, emotionally and spiritually prepared for these experiences, as well as a special gift on March 9th.

The day was sunny and cool as we ventured to the Mount of Beatitudes overlooking the Sea of Galilee. I was walking with Shawna, a kind young woman from our church who I met in the van to the airport. We are busily talking as we walked up the hill to get a full view of the sea. Parts of our group were in front of us, others behind. This was a good hike by my novice standards. Sections of the hill were grassy and rugged, with large stones. The colors were phenomenal. There were hues of green, brown and yellow. As we turned the corner, my heart melted. Tears swelled in my eyes and I was breathless. "What is it?" Shawna asked me. "Are you okay, Debra?"

I looked at Shawna with wet eyes and out came the words, "It's the row of mustard seed trees. They're glorious. I can hardly believe my eyes. My late husband gave me a mustard seed necklace as his first gift to me in middle school. I didn't know the meaning until I began to seriously study the Bible a few years ago." Shawna looked at me with anticipation, and the words slowly poured from my lips. "In the Bible, Matthew 17:20 says, '...if you have faith like a grain of mustard seed...nothing will be impossible for you.'" I then paused and shared with Shawna, "And I can't believe that of all the days for us to visit Mount of Beatitudes and see the rows of yellow mustard seed trees, today is my husband's second anniversary in Heaven."

Somehow, I know God connected Harry and me that day. Sometimes we need to wait and be prepared for God to reveal answers to us. That can take minutes, days, weeks or years. Sometimes we may never get the answer. But we do know that God is in control. He holds the plans to our life. He sets everything in order. It may not be our order, but it's the order that's best for His Kingdom.

I loved Israel. I treasure the gift I received from God on the Mount of Beatitudes. So much so, the picture I took that day is the cover for this book. We returned to New York on March 15, 2020. The world changed overnight. The coronavirus (Covid-19) was starting to spread rapidly throughout the world. Governments were shutting down and quarantining across the globe. The death toll from the virus was rising. As of this writing, we are still in the midst of this deadly virus. It's been devastating. I know God is in control... He is always in control.

Praying for Him to once again rescue us.

"For this is the covenant that I will make with the house of Israel after those days, declares the LORD: I will put my law within them, and I will write it on their hearts. And I will be their God, and they shall be my people." (Jeremiah 31:33, ESV)

CHAPTER 13

Requiring Rest

I was never one to cherish rest. I was brought up in a family that honored and expected hard work. Examples are abundant; however, there are specific role models in this regard I have tried to emulate throughout my life, namely my grandmother Nana Grace, my dad, and my aunt Shirley.

Nana Grace was one amazing woman. She was half Irish, half African American and lived to be 95 years old. She was the matriarch of our family. She married very young (age 16) and had her first child, my mom, at age 17. I loved hearing the stories from my mom and her three sisters on how they really had humble means but never knew it. They went to school with starched clothes, neatly braided hair and clean shoes, and were not allowed to feel like they were less than others. My grandmother did whatever it took to help Papa Charlie, my grandfather, ensure they were able to provide for their family. She would cook, clean, babysit and sew for neighbors whenever possible. Papa worked on the local railroad, lifting heavy steel, and worked through sweltering and freezing temperatures to support his family.

My grandparents lived through the Great Depression, so they were accustomed to living frugally to make ends meet. Papa built the house they raised their four children in, and lived there until the day they both passed away.

And then there's the best dad in the world. My dad commuted to New Jersey for work most of his career, about an hour's drive each way. I watched him rise early each morning and return in the evening to dinner on the table, conversation with his family, and soon off to bed to start all over again. He was a fun and funny dad and loved his faith and family above all else. He was a supervisor at a large automobile company, and after retirement studied and became a deacon in the Catholic Church. He worked extremely hard to support us. I'll never forget when I was about ten years old, we were riding in our car returning home from the store when he looked at me and asked, "Debbie, what do you want to be when you grow up?" At that time, I so enjoyed styling hair on my dolls and family members, or anyone else who would let me experiment. I told him perhaps a hairdresser. He smiled widely and said, "Great, then be the best hairdresser you can possibly be – work hard at it!" My dad was so proud of his four children. His wish for us was to work hard in whatever field we chose, to care about others, and to let God be our guiding light. And we do.

My Aunt Shirley is one of my mom's younger sisters, and she set the example for the women in our family. She was our version of the early 1970s sitcom *Julia*. She was well educated, lived in New York City, worked at one of the larger hospital complexes in New York, and was married to the love of her life. She climbed the corporate ladder at the hospital with grace, dignity and hard work. She was constantly tearing down the stereotypes of what African American women were capable of getting done. I interned one summer at her hospital and was amazed at the respect she received from the doctors, nurses and everyone who worked there. I would stop in the hallways with her as she greeted the custodial staff, and then turn to the head surgeon and greet that person with the same demeanor. It didn't matter what rank they were in the hospital; to her they were simply people trying their best to get the job done.

I often thought it was a special gift to not require much sleep each day. In college, I was the one up early in the morning and rarely got to bed before midnight. When I started my work career, I had to commute into the City, so I was up at the crack of dawn and returned home in the late evening. Before I had children, I would come home, have dinner with my husband, then watch the late news before tucking in. After children, this routine became more and more difficult, as the demands on my time increased exponentially both at work and home. My husband certainly took up the slack at home, and the roles began to reverse quickly after children. He worked nights and filled his days with running our kids to school and church events, cooking dinner, coaching, and handling any projects that were happening at the time in the house. I continued to work steadily, travel more, and get involved with community work. I knew this schedule was taking a toll on my husband and our marriage, but I didn't know how to get off the roller coaster. I felt trapped.

When my son was about eight months old, I had to go on a business trip to London. I set up everything to make it easy for my husband – baby food, doctor numbers, changing clothes and diapers – or so I thought. My mom was an angel. She helped us with the children when they were young. Since my husband worked nights and I worked days, my mom was the one who would leave her house at 6:00 a.m. every workday to come watch our children until my husband came home. She would also help out when I had to travel on business trips. My children were very close to Nana Irene and did look to her as their second mom.

When I returned home from London, my husband shared that he had just arrived home in the morning from work, relieved my mom, and felt overwhelmed. This wasn't the way he had envisioned his life. He was exhausted from work and then had to come home and care for our young son. He missed his wife and expected more time being a family. He told me that he sat down to feed our son his bottle and as he was looking down at him, a tear began to stream down my husband's cheek. Just as he was reaching for a tissue, my little son grabbed my husband's pinky finger and stared at him. My husband knew at that moment that everything would be okay. Looking back on this story, my husband needed rest too. We were so busy doing what we thought was in the best interest of our family, we often missed the most important part – to take care of yourself so you can better care for others. And be mindful of how you spend your time… it's a gift.

My husband and I thought our rest would come when we were both retired, but most of my early retirement days weren't restful for either of us. They were filled with my husband's doctor visits and dialysis treatments, dietary food and drink restrictions, medications and consultations. We were both anxious and nervous, trying to understand our situation. I slowly watched my husband fall into deep despair as his health continued to deteriorate. I felt helpless. It didn't matter how many doctors were involved, or how many phone calls I made to be sure the insurance was picking up all the bills; I couldn't make this situation better.

My mom's younger sister, Aunt Mary, was very astute and realized I needed the kind of help that was far from anything I could get from any other human being. I was not practicing my Catholic faith at the time when she asked if I wanted to join her at her Presbyterian church. I was at a point in my life where I felt something was missing. I could no longer hide this fact from myself. It was difficult for me to actually admit I had abandoned my religion over the years, but I had. I had faith, or thought I did, but it wasn't part of my daily walk in life. I was staring at my life and glancing at God, instead of staring at God and glancing at my life.

I walked into my aunt's Presbyterian church after 55 years of only knowing the Catholic church. It was rather large, with three sections for seating. Right away I noticed there were no statues, or large marble alters, or stained-glass windows. The organ had been replaced by guitars, drums and a piano. It appeared clean, modern and minimalistic. There was no kneeling bench or missalettes. There were several individual cushioned chairs. As we sat waiting for the service to begin, a large screen denoted the countdown for all to see, then out came a pastor with no long robes but neatly dressed in a suit with tie. He looked younger than he actually was, and addressed the congregation with an opening prayer then asked everyone to stand for worship.

And then the music began. This is when all my worries and anxieties came down on me, like I had been struck by lightning. All I had been holding inside was unleashed like a water dam being held back by a brick wall. I began to tear, then cry, then sob. Aunt Mary never said a word, just gently put her arm around me as if to say it's all going to be okay. She handed me a tissue and the music continued to play.

God put me in that church because He knew what I needed. I needed Him. I somehow lost sight of that in trying to be a good wife, mother, daughter, sister, niece, friend, worker. He gave me the guardrails to get through the next step of my journey, and I've been going to the Presbyterian church ever since that first encounter in 2016, joining officially as a member after my husband passed in 2018. I came to realize very quickly that religion is not faith. One must have faith – the belief in God, Jesus and the Holy Spirit. And that needs to be a living thing, not a passive thing. It's one thing to say I'm Catholic, or Baptist, or Presbyterian; it's quite another to say I practice my faith every day to serve God and His kingdom. It's a journey, and it's the most important journey of our lives.

I did find rest in the teaching of the gospel each week at church. I had this new desire to become more educated in my faith. It's always been there since I can remember. However, sometimes it was more active than other times. In my desire to learn more about my faith, I set some goals. One goal was to read the Bible cover to cover – every word, every page. I selected the English Standard Version (ESV) as that seemed to be easier to understand for me. I didn't realize the joy it would bring to read the passages and reflect. Most times, there was a direct correlation to what I was challenged with at the time. It was as though God was calling me to "Read this now." As of this writing, I have completed all 66 books. It took two and a half years – a lifelong blessing indeed. I know I will need to continue to read it over and over again. It's woven into the intricate pattern of life. And at each reading, more is learned.

I also found rest in prayer. I've prayed most of my life; however, I've never prayed harder or more often than during my husband's sickness and now. I'm learning the power of prayer when it's done with raw honesty and love—and most of all, faith.

One day while reading my emails, I noticed one from Proverbs 31 Ministries, a women's Christian organization. I'm not quite sure how or why I received this email. Upon investigating the group, I learned they post a daily devotional, host Bible study classes, teach writing classes, have conferences, and sponsor a host of other events. I signed up for the daily devotional about three years ago. It's helped me tremendously to read these devotionals and incorporate them into my faith journey.

I've also found that meditation can be quite fulfilling. For me, at first it was the ability to be still and listen, but through Bible study I've learned that meditation can be active. A safe place to ask questions, let loose and be free. Your most inner secrets, confessions, desires and wishes can be part of meditation. God already knows the heart and the mind. He wants us to know it too. There is so much power in letting go and cleansing your mind of the day-to-day noise.

I attended the "She Speaks" conference held in North Carolina in 2019 hosted by Proverbs 31 Ministries. My cousin's wife, Kippie, attended with me. Kippie has been a long-standing Christian and wrote her own self-help book for women over twenty years ago. I felt she would really appreciate the focus on both the faith journey and writing at this conference. My cousin Greg joined the trip and we took advantage of being in the area to visit with other family members as well–mainly my niece, Gina and her husband Kevin. During this trip, I was also delighted to get a chance to catch up with my friend Jeanne who lived in the area. Jeanne and I worked for the same firm years ago and had common values regarding faith and family. Jeanne is a living example of what true faith looks like. She was diagnosed with breast cancer many years ago and was in remission for several years. The cancer reappeared in other areas of her body a couple of years ago. She is handling this situation with grace and dignity but foremost with faith. She has taught me (and many others) how one fully surrenders, let go to let God. Jeanne showed up at my hotel lobby and then came by the conference area the next day. It was wonderful as she was able to meet Greg and Kippie. Before Kippie knew about Jeanne's steadfast faith and current battle, she told me there was something very special about Jeanne – she received a connection that was quite unexplainable. Jeanne felt the same about Kippie. When Kippie returned home she had a prayer shawl made for Jeanne. I cannot believe these connections that can only happen through the miraculous grace of God. I live and learn by Jeanne and Kippie. I'm so happy God connected us.

I met Dr. Saundra Dalton-Smith at the She Speaks conference attending her session "Self-Care, Soul-Care for Creatives: Working from a Place of Rest." It was done so well and articulated the seven different modes of rest that may not be at the top of our minds. She's also written a book called *Sacred Rest: Recover Your Life, Renew Your Energy, Restore Your Sanity.* She writes, "Peace came slowly. It was as if God himself breathed a divine exhalation, released new strength into me. I inhaled it. I clung to the moment, needing it to last a little longer.

I needed even more to satisfy my longing for rest. Not a desire for more sleep, but a yearning to be soul-free. Come to think of it, maybe it wasn't that I needed to be filled, but rather I needed to pour out."

I believe the rest I crave is in the arms of the Prince of Peace. But if I keep putting band-aids on my pain, and living each day stressed and striving after the wrong things, how can I have a sense of peace when I haven't spent any time being with the Prince of it? Dr. Dalton-Smith talks about the seven different types of rest in her book, and there were four that particularly resonated with me.

Physical Rest

While we need physical rest to survive, this can come in a myriad of ways. Getting at least eight hours of sleep a night is, of course, one of the best options. But for those like me who may be restless sleepers or prone to insomnia, eight hours might be a tall order. Working on Wall Street required a lot of physical energy, and sometimes I was up at night because of so many obligations due the following day at work. Although I tried to have a consistent bedtime routine, it wasn't always plausible. Now that I'm retired, I've learned how important it is to care for yourself. If I could redo those years, I would have cared for myself more. I would have taken more baths in the evening to relax my body and put it into sleep mode. I would have exercised more to help relieve stress. If I had taken the time to give myself good quality sleep, it would have improved my relationships as a mother, wife and worker.

Mental Rest

God always knows how to care for His children. This is why it's so important to take a day of rest and worship each week. This day isn't necessarily to catch up on physical rest (which can certainly happen), but more for our minds to rest. Just like anything else, our minds need a break from processing information all the time. This is where hobbies come into play. Hobbies help switch our minds from work to recreation. Jesus took time to switch from the work of healing and driving out demons to fulfilling the Father's business. In Luke 5:15-16 (ESV) it says, *"But now even more the report about him went abroad, and great crowds gathered to hear him and to be healed of their infirmities. But he would withdraw to desolate places and pray."* Part of being a follower of Christ is being a good steward of what God has given us. Jesus withdrew to solitary places and prayed so He could re-center Himself and keep His priorities in order. While all the work He was doing for the Kingdom was good, it was important for Him to keep His mind in optimal shape, so He could continue to make the most of the time He had on Earth.

Emotional Rest

I've learned over the years that taking time for emotional rest is particularly important. There are many burdens in this life that can cause stress, anxiety and depression. I wish I had known about emotional rest at an early age. I was an anxious child but never understood it. I worried about things that had a very small chance of ever happening. I still do that today; however, I'm aware of it now, and actively try to relieve my anxieties. Prayer and meditation have been my saving grace here. I need to feel like I can ask for help. I'm learning that I don't need to hide my emotions. I'm at my best being my authentic self.

Spiritual Rest

This is perhaps the most important rest we can obtain for ourselves. Just like any area of life, we need to rest our souls as well as our minds, bodies and emotions. So often, however, this is the place that may be neglected the most. It's so important to build a relationship with God, to understand you are loved and cared for during the best and worse times of your life. Hebrews 12:1 (ESV) says, *"Therefore, since we are surrounded by so great a cloud of witnesses, let us also lay aside every weight, and sin which clings so closely, and let us run with endurance the race that is set before us."*

Truly, I've also found rest in the people I love. There's a special gift when you spend time with others and find joy in their conversations, laughter, stories and dreams. And just as important, when you empathize with them during troubling times and you really feel their pain. Rest continues to be a journey for me. I'm not there yet. I still have issues sleeping in my bed without my husband.

I still worry constantly about the health and happiness of my children. I still wonder if there was anything more I could've done for my husband or Mom when they were here on this earth. I do understand that in order to give to others, we must first be sure we are taking care of ourselves; spiritually, mentally, physically, emotionally, socially and in many other aspects. I do pray that God teaches me how to live for today, learn from yesterday, and plan for tomorrow in a peaceful, restful way.

CHAPTER **14**

Current Events / Conclusion

O n Sunday, January 26, 2020, while driving home from church and enjoying the quiet ride, I began to think about what to pick up for lunch. I reached down to turn on the radio. After a bit of back and forth with different stations, I settled on one of the national news channels. Most of what I was listening to was background noise, as my thoughts were a million miles away. My attention suddenly tuned to a breaking story: a young professional basketball player, a legend, had died in a helicopter crash that morning. It wasn't until later in the news flash they mentioned there were eight other people on board with him. One was his 13-year-old daughter.

I felt my heart ache for the nine individuals on that helicopter. This basketball player was one my husband loved and admired. I couldn't fathom that he lost his life at the age of 41 – and in this way. The biggest pain came in the announcement that his 13-year-old daughter was on that helicopter with him. I've felt the pain of losing a spouse. I couldn't imagine losing a spouse and child at the same time. My mind immediately focused on his wife and I began to pray for all nine individuals who were killed by this tragic crash, and for each of their families. As expected, most of the media focus was on the well-known basketball player and his daughter; however, the loss, pain and grief were the equalizers across all the families involved.

It was a sad way to start off the year. I knew my son would also be upset and this would trigger thoughts of his dad. I couldn't fathom what other tragic events were in front of us. I thought losing this basketball legend, his daughter and the families in this helicopter would move emotions across the globe and bring everyone together. We would all be awakened to the fragility of life. And yes, it did just that – we were shaken. What I didn't expect is that shortly thereafter, there would be a world-wide event even more devastating.

Approximately two months after the basketball player's death, the coronavirus, also known as Covid-19, came on the scene to the general public. This deadly virus spreads quickly through the nose and mouth and to this day has taken more than 585,000 lives in the United States alone. There hasn't been a virus more widespread and deadly for more than a hundred years.

In the midst of dealing with the coronavirus, there was racial unrest across our nation. A 46-year-old African American gentleman was killed during an attempted arrest. A store clerk said he tried to pass a $20 counterfeit bill. One of the police officers knelt on his neck for an extended period of time. The African American gentleman repeatedly said, "I can't breathe." He died.

Protests ensued across the nation after his death. The protesters wanted justice for this gentleman, his family and all people that face discrimination, prejudice and racism, especially African Americans.

To this day, I cannot watch the video that shows the horrible act of this person losing his life in this way. I realized long ago, the moments around someone's death are sacred. Our hope is that they are surrounded by loved ones, not in pain, and at peace. But too many times we see the other side of this where the person is alone, suffering and distraught. This is currently happening to many individuals inflicted with Covid. Due to the ease of spread of the virus, families and friends have been distanced. Many hospital patients are not allowed to be with their families physically and some are even dying alone. It's a painful, tragic result. I find myself praying to God for grace and mercy, to please rid us of this unfathomable virus.

And more recently, in January 2021, there was a riot and violent attack on the 117th United States Congress at the Capitol Building. The storming of the building was the result of some ideologists believing they could change the outcome of the 2020 US presidential election.

I write this at a time when our country and the world is going through social, political and economic unrest. I am deeply concerned with the world as we know it, and what we will leave for our children. But I do have faith, hope and love. I do believe there are major issues in this earthly life that are beyond human beings' ability to eradicate or fully comprehend. These issues must be in our constant prayers. God is God. He knows everything and has the plan for our lives – our earthly life and our eternal life. He has not changed, ever. He's been there when we haven't been. Even if we cannot fully eradicate an issue, we must attempt to do our part to make it as best as it can be within our power. That's expected and that's Christianity.

I know how it feels to have a blessed life. To go forward with a happy heart, deep family ties, solid friendships. My life has been full of awe, wonder and love. My life has also been full of sadness, loss and pain at times. In my faith journey, I've discovered it has to be this way in order for it to be a full life. I sat down to write this book thirty years ago. I would get upset with myself for not getting through it. I now know that it was to be written on His time, not my time. Even more significant, it's His story, not mine. It's the life God's given me – the wonder and the joy along with the challenges and the defeats, all of it. You see, we have to be thankful for the good in life. It should be cherished and held tight – it's a blessing. But life isn't just made up of *only good things*…there'll be heartache and pain too. Why? Because this brings us closer to understanding who we are, who God intended us to be. And as hurtful as it is to go through challenges in life, it brings us closer to God…always.

> *"Jesus said to His disciples: 'I have said these things to you, that in me you may have peace. In the world you will have tribulation. But take heart; I have overcome the world.'" (John 16:33, ESV)*

About the Author

Debra Baker is a "Christian on a mission," a dedicated mother to two adult children, and a retiree from the financial services industry since 2016, after nearly 35 years in the business. She held several leadership positions across four major Wall Street firms focusing on finance, risk and analytics.

Debra graduated magna cum laude from Niagara University in upstate New York with a B.S. in Economics. She is a former board director for both the Women's Bond Club (WBC) in New York City, and later served as a board director and subsequent chairperson for YWCA of the City of New York. Debra has been a participant in industry recognized programs and has been quoted in several industry related publications relating to global risk services. She was recognized in the Global Custodian "rising star" publication in 2005. She was also a founding member and executive steering committee member for a women's network launched by a major Wall Street firm. In 2011, Debra completed Harvard's Best Practices for Leadership seminar. In 2016, she was named one of the "Top 25 Black Women in Business" by the Network Journal. In 2021, she published her long-awaited memoir, *Only Good Things.*

Debra was born and raised in the beautiful Hudson Valley region of New York. She enjoys spending time with her faith journey, her two adult children, Harry III and Courtney, extended family members and friends, and their pup, Frenchy Paris. Hobbies include charity work, writing, golf, and watching the news as a favorite pastime.

Debra A. Baker
Christian, Mother, Author,
Retired from Financial Services

Works Cited

Dr. Saundra Dalton-Smith:

Self-Care, Soul-Care for Creatives: Working from a Place of Rest. Proverbs 31 She Speaks Conference, July 2019, North Carolina.

Sacred Rest: Recover Your Life, Renew Your Energy, Restore Your Sanity. Faithwords, 1st Edition, December 19, 2017. Book Preview on Google website.

Saint Teresa of Calcutta (formally Mother Teresa) commencement address. Niagara University, May 1982, Niagara Falls NY.

The ESV® Bible (The Holy Bible, English Standard Version®). Copyright 2001 by Crossway, a publishing ministry of Good News Publishers. Used by permission. All rights reserved.

The Holy Bible, New International Version®, NIV®, Copyright 1973, 1978, 1984, 2011 by Biblica Inc.™. Used by permission. All rights reserved worldwide.

CPSIA information can be obtained
at www.ICGtesting.com
Printed in the USA
BVHW020952100721
611456BV00023B/452